SEABOARD
AIR LINE
Color Guide to Freight and Passenger Equipment

To start our book *Seaboard Air Line Color Guide to Freight and Passenger Equipment*, here is an excellent view of the north end of the Seaboard Hermitage shops in Richmond, Va., in April of 1960. Located just down from the Richmond, Fredricksburg and Potomac's Acca Yard, Hermitage appeared to be a continuation of that yard. It was a small, cramped facility, with the longest tracks only 3000 feet long, but it served its owner well. Usually, through trains were simply picked up off the RF&P with very little need for switching. Apparent in this view are Baldwin switchers, E-7s for passenger service, and Geeps for freight service, each in its own paint scheme. Notice the high-sided gondola in the front, along with the covered hopper and the PS-1 boxcar, all indicative of the type of freight the SAL handled.

(*Wiley Bryan, Warren Calloway collection*)

Paul Faulk

Published by
Morning Sun Books, Inc.
9 Pheasant Lane
Scotch Plains, NJ 07076

Library of Congress
Catalog Card No. 98-065946

First Printing
ISBN 1-58248-001-X

Color separation and printing by
The Kutztown Publishing Co., Inc.
Kutztown, Pennsylvania

Dedication
To Dad. This is the book you never wrote.

Acknowledgments

This is my first book and I'm quite proud of it. It is a labor of love and a dream come true. However, I had a lot of help, so I am honored to acknowledge those who worked with me to make my dream a reality. First, I'd like to thank those folks whose slides or collections are featured in this book. These are G. H. Anderson, Ken Ardinger, the late Don Ball, the late George Berisso, S. Bogen, Craig Bossler, the late Wiley Bryan, Warren Calloway, Paul Coe, Lon Coone, Eugene Van Dusen, George Eichelberger, Bill Folsom, Jim Gibson, Larry Goolsby, Bob Graham, Emery Gulash, Jim Hamilton, Matt Herson, Stan Jackowski, K. B. King, Jim Kinkaid, Joe Klaus, Joe Kmetz, Owen Leander, Greg Michels, Norman C. Miller, Joseph Oates, Ron Plazzotta, Dr. Art Peterson, Robert Reisweber, Howard Robins, R. A. Selle, August Staebler, R. Stone, John Szaharzhart, Olev Taremae, C. A. Thomas, Paul C. Winters, Bob Yanosey, Richard Yaremko, and Chuck Yungkurth of Rail Data Services. To each and every one of you, I give my profound appreciation, for this is truly your book.

Next, I would like to thank those individuals that assisted in the preparation of the manuscript and captions. These included Denis Blake, Warren Calloway, George Eichelberger, Larry Goolsby, Jim Kinkaid, Joseph Oates, Howard Robins and Allen Stanley of Railroad Data Exchange. A special thanks goes to George and Howard for giving up a Saturday in the holiday season to preview the manuscript. I'd like to acknowledge the support of the Atlantic Coast Line and Seaboard Air Line Historical Society, who endorsed the project from the beginning and assisted in locating slides and other materials. Those interested in the history of these two unique Southeastern railroads are strongly encouraged to inquire about membership in care of the Society at Box 325, Valrico, Fla., 33595-0325.

Of course, thanks have to go to publisher Bob Yanosey of Morning Sun Books for conceiving the idea for this book, for asking me to do it, and for his encouragement and support until it was completed. Any errors that were made were mine, and not attributable to the contributors. Last, but not least, this book would not have been possible without the patient understanding and support of my family: my wife Linda, who is patient with my hobby, my son Stephen, who accompanies Dad on train trips, my Mom and late Father, who encouraged my interest growing up, and my in-laws Laura and Richard Harris, who continue to encourage my interest.

SEABOARD AIR LINE

TABLE OF CONTENTS

SEABOARD AIR LINE

Color Guide to Freight and Passenger Equipment

The Seaboard Air Line Railroad was a 4200 mile rail system serving the six Southeastern states of Virginia, North Carolina, South Carolina, Georgia, Alabama, and Florida. Located between rivals Atlantic Coast Line and Southern, it had the unenviable position of usually having the poorer route to most of the same southeastern markets as its two competitors. This forced the railroad to adopt a policy of using its other assets to compete effectively against its two larger neighbors.

The Seaboard Air Line *Railway* was formed in 1900 from the end to end amalgamation of a number of regional lines. Yet, the road can trace its beginnings to the dawn of railroading in the United States, with its earliest predecessor having been chartered in 1832. While the association was initially created to provide through, or "air line" service between Portsmouth, Va. and Atlanta, Ga., lines to Richmond and Miami were added later by a consortium of wealthy financiers to create the main line of the railroad. It was the line to Miami, completed in 1928, the year after the Florida boom ended, that plunged the railway into bankruptcy. This gave the road the dubious distinction of being the first bankrupt railroad of the Great Depression. The following years were lean, but the road was able to survive, due to the skillful management of its receivers. It was noted for its pioneering spirit, being one of the first railroads to use articulated locomotives for fast freight service, to use diesels on passenger trains, and to use CTC. It also ran the first lightweight passenger train in the South, the SILVER METEOR. As one of the railroad's receivers so aptly put it, "The Seaboard was too poor to have anything but the very best." The Second World War brought a heavy influx of traffic to the road, and finally allowed it to re-organize and emerge from bankruptcy in 1945 as the Seaboard Air Line *Railroad*.

The following years resulted in a number of improvements. These included the expansion of CTC, the installation of double track between Hialeah and Miami, improvements in yard and shop facilities, and the modernization of the physical plant. 1953 dieselized the road, and 1954 saw the completion of a modern, state-of-the art hump yard at Hamlet, N. C., the only one on the system. The headquarters were located in Richmond, Va., where they were moved from Portsmouth, Va. in 1958. Locomotive back shops were located at West Jacksonville, Fla., with other facilities at Hamlet, N. C., Savannah, Ga., Atlanta, Ga., Tampa, Fla., and Hialeah, Fla. The main car shops were located at Portsmouth, Va., with additional facilities at Hamlet, N. C., Savannah, Ga., West Jacksonville, Fla., and Tampa, Fla. The wheel and axle shop was located at Hamlet, N. C. The Seaboard owned two subsidiaries, the Tavares and Gulf, a Florida short line, and the Gainesville Midland, which it acquired in 1959. In 1958, after several years of control, it merged the Macon, Dublin and Savannah into the system.

The 1960's would continue the trend of modernization and development started in the 1950's. While this would be the last decade of the railroad's operation, it would be one that would see the road really come into its own. Improvements in operations, technology, and efficiency impacted the bottom line, such that in 1966, the last full year of operation, the profits of the road exceeded that of its one-time rival, the Atlantic Coast Line. On August 18, 1960, the shareholders of the Atlantic Coast Line and Seaboard Air Line approved the merger of the two roads. However, objections and court cases kept the merger from becoming a reality until July 1, 1967, when the two roads finally consummated their union to become the Seaboard Coast Line. Thus, an era passed, and the road that ran "Through the Heart of the South" became history. Today, what remains of this railroad is a part of CSX Corporation.

These passenger cars were part of a mail and express train. In this view, from right to left, is the end of an RPO car, a 1300 series horse express car, SAL's only lightweight baggage car 6070, combine 272, and one of the ex-C&O lightweight coaches. These cars are shown crossing the Appomattox River at Petersburg, Va. in June of 1967. (Dr. Art Peterson)

Passenger Equipment

The Seaboard Air Line was a major player in the Northeast to Florida passenger traffic. The road distinguished itself with its premier passenger trains, the SILVER METEOR and SILVER STAR, running between New York and Florida, and the SILVER COMET, running between New York and Birmingham, Ala. The road boasted a first class, winter only, all-Pullman train, the ORANGE BLOSSOM SPECIAL, running between New York and Florida. However, this train was dropped in 1953 before the equipment was changed to lightweight cars. By the beginning of the Second World War, all of its first class passenger trains ran with diesels. The road quickly established a reputation for fast passenger trains providing excellent service. The first class trains were supported by a number of local, mail and express trains, some of which ran equally fast.

Early photographs of SAL passenger cars show vestibuled wooden cars with six wheel trucks, lettered for the ATLANTA SPECIAL, an early Portsmouth, Va. to Atlanta, Ga. train. The first steel cars were purchased around 1913. Cars were added as the need arose and finances permitted, usually in small lots of five to ten. Although well known for its use of lightweight equipment (34.9%), the most of the passenger cars were heavyweights (48.7%), with express cars, in the form of modified box cars, refrigerator cars and Mark III flat cars, providing the remainder (16.3%) of the passenger car roster. An analysis of the heavyweight roster in 1966 shows a heavy concentration on postal and baggage-express cars to support the still lucrative mail and express business. This type composed 60.5% of the heavyweight passenger car roster. Coaches followed at 22.3%, with combines next at 9.4%, business cars at 3.5%, and other types as diners, sleepers, and lounge cars providing the balance. Pullman was the favored heavyweight car builder, providing 56.6% of the roster, with American Car and Foundry next at 21.2%, Pressed Steel Car at 17.2%, and other builders such as Bethlehem Steel and General American providing the balance. Over the years, these cars were modernized with the addition of air conditioning, resulting in new rooflines and wider sealed windows. Some cars were rebuilt, such as diners into express cars and sleepers into coaches. Heavyweight cars were painted the traditional Pullman green with extended Railroad roman gold lettering. This remained unchanged until 1947, when the color of the lettering was changed to 8" high, dulux gold, and the style was changed to match the lightweight passenger car lettering. Some cars carried other paint schemes, as the maroon and gray cars assigned to the ORANGE BLOSSOM SPECIAL, the two tone gray heavyweight sleepers purchased from Pullman in 1948, and the cars temporarily assigned to lightweight trains in the 1940's.

The Seaboard Air Line's first purchase of lightweight equipment came in 1936, when the road bought six "American Flyer" type coaches from the Pullman Company. These were painted Pullman green with gold lettering, like the heavyweight equipment. The next purchase of lightweight equipment came in 1939, when the road bought stainless steel cars from Budd for its new train, the SILVER METEOR. Initially, the SILVER METEOR was a coach train that served both coasts of Florida on an alternating day basis. The next year, additional equipment was purchased to allow the popular train to serve both coasts daily. When the train's popularity forced service to be expanded to add sleepers, lightweight sleepers could not be obtained due to the restrictions of World War II. As a result, the train ran with a mixed consist of lightweight and heavyweight equipment. The heavyweight cars regularly assigned to this and other lightweight trains were "shadowlined" or painted gray, in an effort to blend them in. The conclusion of the Second World War and the subsequent boom in passenger travel resulted in the addition of two new trains. Lightweight equipment was delivered for the SILVER STAR and SILVER COMET in 1947 and 1948. However, it would be 1949 before the SAL was finally able to obtain lightweight sleepers from Pullman, due to a huge backlog of orders. An analysis of the lightweight roster in 1966 shows this equipment existed to service the long distance trains. Coaches composed 40% of the roster, with sleepers following at 24%, diners at 13%, baggage-dormitory cars at 7%, observation cars at 4%, and other odd types providing the balance. Budd was the favored lightweight builder at 65.3%, with Pullman providing most of the sleeping cars and some other cars at 31.7%, and American Car and Foundry providing the remaining 3%. Lettering on lightweight cars was 8" high and black in an extended, condensed style similar to that used by the CB&Q.

The construction of the Interstate highway system and the increase in airline travel signaled the beginning of the end for passenger service. While the Seaboard continued to make money on passenger service, by 1955, this increased competition was being felt. The road responded by modernizing service on its flagship SILVER METEOR in the form of six new 11 double bedroom sleepers and 3 unique, glass topped lounge cars, which would be its last new passenger cars. Other passenger car acquisitions came when the SAL bought some ex-C&O cars, built for the stillborn CHESSIE, and some ex-FEC cars, obtained in 1965 after the strike-bound FEC quit the passenger business.

There was a passenger car classification system, but it was abandoned prior to the acquisition of lightweight equipment. It is listed below:

> AP - RPO car
> DC - Diner
> EX - Express
> MB - Mail, Baggage
> PB - Passenger, Baggage
> PC - Passenger, Coach

The car type letter was followed by a number, which was generally assigned in order of purchase. For example, a DC6 diner was purchased before a DC7, and so on.

Here is a shot of the head end of a local freight, featuring RS-3 1639 as power. The gondola following the locomotive is not a Seaboard car, but from neighbor ACL, with whom the SAL merged in 1967 to create the Seaboard Coast Line. This train is shown in Sarasota, Fla. in June of 1962. (Norman C. Miller, George Eichelberger collection)

Freight Equipment

Most of the Seaboard's freight traffic were commodities generated in the South and associated with it, such as pulpwood, paper, lumber, gypsum products, kaolin, phosphate, aggregates, chemicals, fiber and cloth products, and farm commodities as feed, fertilizer, and produce. There was steel traffic from Birmingham, Ala. and manufacturing traffic from the emerging manufacturing centers of the South. Perishable traffic was present in high volumes, but it had only a modest effect on the freight car roster, as SAL refrigerator cars were leased or borrowed from Fruit Grower's Express as a result of its membership in that organization. The SAL also had considerable business hauling other food items as coffee, beer, orange juice, poultry, and canned fruits and vegetables. The railroad started using piggyback service in 1959, as an attempt to keep its market share of the perishable traffic being lost to trucks. Autorack traffic was added in 1960, which consisted of vehicles bound from factories to southeastern distribution centers. The railroad excelled in running priority traffic on tight schedules, thereby maintaining its competitive edge.

An analysis of the freight car roster in 1966 reveals that the Seaboard was primarily a boxcar road. This type comprised 35% of the total roster, followed by gondolas at 17%, open hoppers with 15%, pulpwood cars at 12%, covered hoppers, at 11%, flats at 2.5%, and refrigerator cars at 2.5%. Pullman provided the bulk of the freight cars, at 45% of the roster, followed by American Car and Foundry at 13%, Bethlehem at 9.4%, Magor at 5.5%, Greenville at 4.3%, and Pressed Steel at 2%. The remainder of the

builders, including Thrall, Bethlehem/Pullman, General Steel, General American and others, comprised less than 2% each. A significant number of the hoppers, both open and covered, were actually phosphate cars, used in the huge "Bone Valley" mining district near Tampa, Fla. While some of these cars did venture outside that area, most of them spent their entire service careers in and around "Bone Valley." The Seaboard, unlike neighbor Southern, preferred not to buy or modify cars to fit the needs of a particular customer, nor were they particularly innovative in design. Instead, they generally chose to buy large groups of cars of a proven design, equip them with good features, such as cushioned underframes, load restraints, and roller bearings, and dedicate them to a particular shipper to allow maximum flexibility of the fleet.

Equipment was painted in a manner that was conservative, yet appealing. The herald was a concentric circle containing the name with a red heart containing the slogan, "Through the Heart of the South." This first appeared in 1932, in the 40" size on ARA boxcars 17000-17999. In 1944, the size of the herald was increased to 56", but the smaller herald continued to be used. Boxcars were painted in boxcar red with white graphics. The Seaboard, like the Santa Fe, was quick to recognize the value of boxcar sides as "rolling billboards," so starting in 1937, they added slogans advertising their name trains. The table below lists where these slogans where originally used, along with the dates used:

Slogan	Dates Used	Number Series	Dates on cars
Route of the Orange Blossom Special			
	1937-1954	14000-14999	ptd 1952-1954
		17000-17999	rptd after 1937
Route of the Robert E. Lee			
	1937-1944	10000-10199	new in 1938
		11000-11999	new in 1938
		22000-22199	new in 1942
Route of the Silver Meteor			
	1944-1963	17000-19699	rptd after 1944
Route of Courteous Service			
	1944-1963	9100-9149	new in 1947
		19700-19999	new in 1945
		21000-21999	new in 1959
		21700-21999	new in 1959
		22000-22949	rptd after 1947
		23000-23099	new in 1948
		24000-24299	new in 1948
		24500-24799	new in 1951
		25000-25299	new in 1952
		27000-27499	new in 1955
Route of the Silver Comet			
	1947-1963	11700-11999	rptd after 1947
		22000-22199	rptd after 1947
		24300-24499	new in 1948
		24800-24999	new in 1951
Route of the Silver Star			
	1947-1963	25300-25499	new in 1952

Other boxcars had these slogans, especially after repainting, so the table above should not be regarded as absolute. The slogans were later replaced with the railroad name in 24" billboard lettering, first in block style, about 1963, and next in Railroad Roman,

in late 1964. The Seaboard tended to identify cars with specialized equipment with different paint schemes. Boxcars with roof insulation or other equipment featured a silver or gray scheme with black and red graphics. Cushioned underframe boxcars featured a dark green paint scheme with yellow lettering. These attractive cars, known to the crews as "Green Hornets," had three paint schemes. The first style, used in 1962, featured the slogan "Cushioned Underframe" in 16" block letters over the slogan "Perfect Product Protection." A 40" herald with the 9" roadname underneath appeared on the right side of the car. The next version, created about 1963, used the railroad name in 24" block lettering over the 16" "Cushioned Underframe," with the 56" herald on the right side of the car. The last version, created in late 1964, changed the lettering style to Railroad Roman.

As for other freight cars, gondolas were painted boxcar red with a 30" herald. Flat cars and pulpwood cars were also painted red with the name in 9" high Railroad Roman. An exception here was the cushioned underframe bulkhead flats used for wallboard, which were painted green with yellow lettering. Hoppers were painted boxcar red and featured the 56" herald. Newer hoppers omitted the herald, featuring the 9" name. The last lot of woodchip hoppers featured the name in 24" Railroad Roman lettering. Covered hoppers and phosphate cars were painted gray, with the 9" name in black. The Magor cars, 35805-35899, featured a 40" herald with the 6" roadname underneath. The pneumatic flow hopper cars featured the 24" block road name in black, while the later PS-2 three bay hoppers and ACF Centerflow cars featured the 24" Railroad Roman road name in black. Cabooses were bright red with white graphics with a 40" herald. The newer extended vision cabooses omitted the large herald, due to lack of room on the sides, but featured a 21" herald on the cupola side. Beginning in 1953, safety slogans were added on the sides, keyed to the last digit of the car number. Maintenance of Way equipment was painted Pullman green, with gold 9" Railroad Roman lettering. Leased Fruit Grower's Express refrigerator cars and insulated boxcars were painted in their livery, which was yellow with boxcar red ends and silver roof, with only the reporting marks indicating the lessee. Autoracks were boxcar red with white graphics, though some cars, probably with cushioned underframes, were painted dark green with yellow graphics. As will be seen, there were a multitude of variations in the freight car lettering, as individual shops tended to follow their own standards at times.

The Seaboard did have a Freight Car Classification System, but it was abandoned around 1951. Although newer cars were never assigned a class, its use continued on repainted equipment, even up until the merger. The system is explained below:

A - Auto box	H - Open hopper
AF - Automobile Furniture	P - Phosphate hopper
B - Box	(open and covered)
C - Covered Hopper	R - Wood rack (Pulpwood cars)
F - Flat	S - Stock car
G - Gondola	V - Ventilated boxcar
	CC - caboose

Like passenger equipment, the car type letter was followed by a number, which was generally assigned in order of purchase, as a B6 boxcar was purchased before a B7, and so on.

SAL PV *Virginia*

◄ Every railroad had office cars. Executives used these cars for travel and entertaining. Here is a nice shot of the SAL private car *Virginia*, which was built in 1924 by Pullman. It is listed as having capacity for 6 persons in three compartments with three toilets. Shown at Richmond, Va. on September 5, 1966. *(Matt Herson)*

SAL PV *Southland*

◄ The *Southland,* originally built as a parlor car in 1914 for the ATSF, was converted into the office car *Birmingham* by the SAL in 1948. In 1953, the name was changed to the *Southland*. In service, it was assigned to the president of the railroad. It had the capacity of three persons in three staterooms with three toilets. It is shown here in Raleigh, N. C. on the rear of train #9, date unknown.

(Warren Calloway, Paul Faulk collection)

SAL PV *Richmond*

▼ The office car *Richmond* was originally built 1911 by Pullman as the *Winchester*. It was purchased in 1917 by the SAL and converted to the office car *Portsmouth*, becoming the *Richmond* by 1920 after a couple of other name changes. It had the capacity of 5 persons in three compartments. Shown in its namesake city of Richmond, Va. on September 5, 1966. *(Matt Herson)*

HEAD END EQUIPMENT

HEAVYWEIGHT MAIL AND BAGGAGE CARS

SAL MB 89, series 80-91, class MB8

▲ Pressed Steel Car Co. built this mail and baggage car in 1915. This car had a body length of 70' with a single 4' baggage door on each side and a 30' mail compartment. At some point in time, this car was modernized, and the original clerestory roof was modified to the "turtle back" roof as shown. This car was the "typical" RPO car, and like most mail cars, had a spartan interior with a solid partition between the baggage and mail sections. Shown in Atlanta, Ga. in June of 1968. *(Howard Robins)*

SAL MB 106, series 104-109, class MB8

▼ Here is another modernized mail and baggage car, built by American Car and Foundry in 1924. This car had a body length of 70' with a pair of 5'6" baggage doors on each side and a 30' mail compartment. This is the gray paint scheme that was created to allow older, heavyweight cars to blend in with the newer lightweight equipment. This car is shown on the eve of the SCL merger in June of 1967 at the Atlanta, Ga. Union Station. *(Howard Robins)*

7

SAL MB 113, series 112-113, class MB8

▼ This car is a mail and baggage car built by American Car and Foundry in 1925. *This car* has a body length of 70', with a pair of 5'6" baggage doors and a 15' mail compartment. This car, like the preceding cars, was modernized at some point and re-painted into the gray scheme. Made surplus after the mail left the rails, these cars found their way into maintenance of way service or were scrapped. Shown at Waycross, Ga. on April 21, 1973. *(George Eichelberger)*

SAL MA 150, series 150-155, class AP4

▲ This is a true RPO car, with no baggage or express section, meant for handling mail only. This car was built by Pressed Steel Car Co. in 1925, and retained its "as built" appearance for all of its service life. The car was 60' long, and had two 2'10" doors on each side. Note the mail catchers on each door for picking up mail on the fly. Shown in Hamlet, N. C. on February 16, 1961. *(Wiley Bryan, Ken Ardinger collection)*

SAL BEM 326, series 321-327, class EX5

▼ This is a 70' baggage car, built in 1916 by Pressed Steel Car Company. This car has no facilities for employees, and has one pair of doors ten feet wide, and another door four feet wide. Virtually a shell on wheels, cars like this were used for handling any type of express shipment that needed the fast schedules of a passenger train. Shown at Columbus, Ohio in PRR train #14 on December 1, 1962. *(Paul C. Winters)*

SAL BEM 346, series 342-347

▶ This car originally built by Pullman in 1913 as a diner numbered 998, was converted to a baggage car by the Portsmouth shops in 1932. The car is unusual in that it has a single personnel door on the end of this side only, probably a relic from its days as a diner that had some utility in its new function. The first baggage door is a single four foot door, while the last one is a pair of four foot doors. The car itself was 72'4" long. Shown on the PRR in Columbus, Ohio on December 19, 1962. *(Paul C. Winters)*

SAL BEM 353

▲ Here is another baggage car, a lot of one, which was originally built as the Postal Baggage car 261 by Pressed Steel Car Company in 1915. It was converted to a standard express car by the Portsmouth shops in 1953, and modernized some time after that. The clean turtleback roof is a result of that modernization. This car was 73'9" long and had six foot and eight foot door openings. Shown in Tampa, Fla. at Tampa Union Station in May of 1969. *(Joseph Oates)*

SAL BEM 368, series 360-391

▼ These cars were 60' baggage cars built by Pullman in 1926 with four and eight foot door openings. They retained the same numbers all of their service lives. A few of these cars where modernized, but this particular car retains its original appearance. Shown in St. Petersburg, Fla. in April 1968. *(Paul Coe)*

SAL BEM 389, series 360-391

▼ Here is another one of the 60' baggage cars showing the roof detail. Note the ACL baggage car still in purple paint coupled to this car, the Southern transfer run in the background with the pair of RS-3s, and all those neat, 1960's era freight cars. Shown in Atlanta, Ga. in June of 1968 after the SCL merger. *(Howard Robins)*

HEAD END EQUIPMENT

LIGHTWEIGHT BAGGAGE CARS

10

SAL BEM 6070

▲ Originally built by American Car and Foundry in 1950 as the FEC 501, this car was among the cars sold to the SAL in 1965. As such, it was the only lightweight, full baggage car on the railroad. Since the baggage dormitory cars were usually adequate for the long distance trains, this car usually was assigned to local trains that had heavy express needs. Shown in Tampa, Fla. in July of 1968.

(Joseph Oates)

HEAD END EQUIPMENT

HEAVYWEIGHT HORSE EXPRESS CARS

SAL BH 13xx, series 1300-1314

▼ This is a horse express car, built by American Car and Foundry in 1926. As the name implies, these cars were used for the transport of thorough-bred horses too valuable to ride in stock cars. These animals would have to be moved periodically between their owners' farms and the racetracks or training tracks in Hialeah, Fla. or Camden, S. C. Originally named for famous esquestians, these cars were 74'9" long and had three doors on each side, with the two end doors being 5'6" wide and the center door being 7' wide. Shown crossing the Appomattox River in Petersburg, Va. in June of 1967. *(Dr. Art Peterson)*

HEAD END EQUIPMENT

HEAVYWEIGHT BAGGAGE DORMITORY CARS

SAL CSB 184, series 180-184

▲ Pullman originally built this heavyweight baggage dormitory car in 1926 as the club car *Barren Hills*. It was converted by the SAL in 1946 and assigned to the road's premier all-Pullman winter train, the ORANGE BLOSSOM SPECIAL. The car had a 24' baggage section with 5' doors, and was able to sleep 20 crewmembers in berths of two and three tiers. The car is shown in the later gray scheme at St. Petersburg, Fla. in January of 1968.

(Paul Coe)

SAL CSB 184, series 180-184

▼ Here is a vintage view of the coach yards at the Washington, DC Union Station, in April of 1953. While the whole view shows some really neat equipment, what is of interest here is SAL heavyweight baggage dormitory car 184 in the foreground. Color shots of this paint scheme, which was the last paint scheme used on the ORANGE BLOSSOM SPECIAL, are rare. Here, a Washington Terminal RS-1 switches this car.

(Paul Coe)

11

HEAD END EQUIPMENT

LIGHTWEIGHT BAGGAGE DORMITORY CARS

SAL CSP 6004, series 6003-6005

▲ This car is a baggage-dormitory-passenger car built by Budd in 1940. These cars had a 22'7" baggage section, with space for 15 crew members and 18 passengers. These cars were generally assigned to the long distance passenger trains, where they provided sleeping quarters for the porters and dining car staff. This beauty is shown in St. Petersburg, Fla. in December of 1970. *(Howard Robins)*

SAL CSP 6004, series 6003-6005

◄ Here is another view of the same car, this time from the baggage end and opposite side. Shown in Tampa, Fla. in June of 1969. These cars were among the first cars of this type, ordered to augment the SILVER METEOR. Note the trucks with the brake cylinders hung on the rear extension. The baggage door at the very end of the car is typical of baggage-dormitory cars. *(Joseph Oates)*

SAL CSB 6057, series 6057-6058

▼ Here is a baggage dormitory car originally built by Budd in 1939. These cars featured 26' of baggage space with the remainder of the car providing space for 24 crew members. This car was originally built for the FEC as their *Halifax River*. Compared to the previous car, the baggage door on this car is set back from the end a bit. Shown here in West Lake Wales, Fla. in February of 1968. *(Paul Coe)*

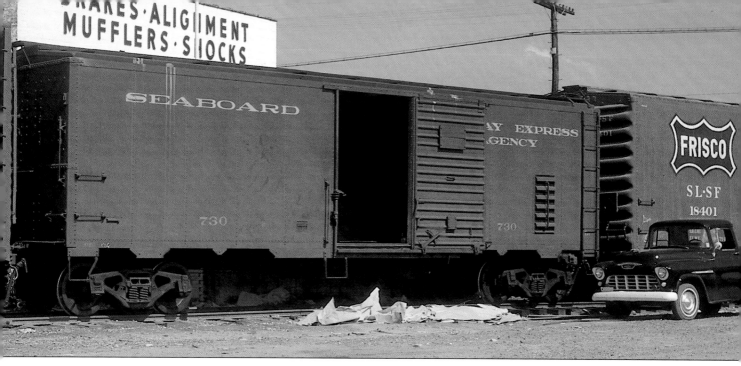

SAL BX 730, series 700-754

▲ The Seaboard, like most other railroads, handled considerable express business in its passenger trains. To assist with this business, the road converted boxcars to express service by adding high speed trucks and steam lines. These cars were originally built in 1937 by Pullman, and converted by the Portsmouth shops in 1943-1945. They were rated at 50 tons and painted passenger car green with passenger lettering. Note the vent in the side. Shown at Rome, Ga. in August of 1965. *(Bill Folsom collection)*

SAL BX 744, series 700-754

▼ Here is another shot of a SAL express car. This car carries the later SAL passenger lettering, unusual on these cars, which is barely discernible through the coating of grime. Cars like this handled all sorts of time sensitive cargo. Express business was fairly lucrative for the SAL, so much so that they felt the need to convert an additional 15 cars, 756-770, in 1963. Shown at Milwaukee, Wis. in October of 1966. *(Ron Plazzotta)*

13

SAL BX 755

▲ General American Car originally built this car in 1930 as a 50'
refrigerator express car. It was converted from 3626 to handle ice
cream in 1958, at which time the insulation was increased, the
door was changed to a plug door, and the ice compartment was
removed. Then, in 1962, it was re-assigned to general express
service and renumbered. It is shown here in Atlanta, Ga. on July
17, 1966. *(Larry Goolsby)*

SAL BR 3625, series 3600-3649

▼ Originally built in 1930 by General American Car, these cars
were 50' long with a 40'10" interiors. Originally they had wood
sides and curved roofs, but several were modernized. Over the
years their ranks were decimated, until only eight remained on
the roster by 1966. Apparently, the SAL leased the cars to
Railway Express, which may explain the REX lettering shown
here. These cars did have SAL lettering at one time. Shown at
Tampa, Fla. in March of 1969. *(Joseph Oates)*

14

COMBINES

HEAVYWEIGHT COMBINES

SAL CA 271, series 271-276, class PB7

▲ Built by American Car and Foundry in 1924, this combine was 73'10" long with a 30' baggage compartment with two 4' baggage doors. It was air conditioned by Pullman in 1934. These cars had two passenger compart- ments, one smoking and one main, for a total seating capacity of 36. There was also a room with a desk for the conductor. Shown at Wildwood, Fla. in March of 1966. *(Rail Data Services)*

SAL CA 280, series 277-282, class PB7

▲ The Seaboard returned to American Car and Foundry in 1926 for another six cars that were virtually identical to those in the previous series. With their interior layout and conductor's offices, these cars were frequently assigned to secondary passenger trains, which could put their facilities to good use. Shown in St. Petersburg, Fla. in October, 1969, after the SCL merger.

(Paul Coe)

SAL CA 282, series 277-282, class PB7

▶ Here is another view of this series of cars, this time from the other side. Note the two small windows at the end nearest the baggage door. This is were the lavatory was located. The duct work on the roof, present on this side only, shows how the car was air conditioned. Shown in the gray paint scheme in St. Petersburg, Fla. in April of 1967.

(Paul Coe)

SAL CA 283

▲ Pressed Steel Car Co. originally built this car in 1925 for the Bessemer and Lake Erie as their car 21. It was acquired by the SAL in 1944, probably to handle the heavy influx of wartime traffic. It was 76' 3" long with a 29'10" baggage compartment with 6' doors. It seated 40 people, and, like most other combines, it had a conductor's room. There was no air conditioning, which probably lead to the car's retirement by 1966. Shown in Atlanta, Ga. in December of 1963. (*Howard Robins*)

16

COMBINES
LIGHTWEIGHT COMBINES

SAL CA 288, series 285-288, class PB8

▼ Satisfied with the lightweight Pullman "American Flyer" coaches purchased the year before, the SAL went back to Pullman Bradley at Worchester, Mass. in 1937 for these combines. These cars were 77'10" long, with three compartments and a conductor's office. The baggage compartment was 27'11" long and had 4' doors. The smoking compartment had 20 seats, while the main compartment had 28 seats. Originally delivered with pillars in the windows and side skirting, these were removed in later years as the cars were modernized. Shown in Ocala, Fla. in May 1968. (*Ron Plazzotta*)

COACHES

HEAVYWEIGHT COACHES

SAL PB 586, series 581-590, class PC7

▲ These cars were purchased from Pressed Steel Car Company in 1914. Billed as day coaches, they were 72'4" long with both a smoking compartment and a passenger compartment. They had a total capacity of 64 seats. These cars were modernized by Pullman in 1936 and 1944, at which time sealed windows and air conditioning was added, thus altering the original appearance of these cars. By 1966, only this car remained on the roster. Shown in Hamlet, N. C. in March of 1961 *(Wiley Bryan, Ken Ardinger collection)*

SAL PB 808, series 807-814, class PC9

▲ Built by American Car and Foundry in 1926, these cars carried 48 seats in two compartments. They were 72'4" long. This particular car was modernized in 1954 at Portsmouth, at which time air conditioning and the wider windows were added. Shown in the gray paint scheme, this car awaits the end at Tampa, Fla. in the David J. Joseph scrap line. *(Joseph Oates)*

SAL PB 811, series 807-814, class PC9

▼ Here is another coach from the same series, but this one is in the standard green paint scheme. This is a nice broadside shot, made at St. Petersburg, Fla. in June of 1969, after the SCL merger. Modernized with air conditioning and having six wheeled trucks for a good ride, these cars lasted until the advent of Amtrak on secondary trains. *(Paul Coe)*

SAL PB 819, series 815-828, class PC9

▲ The SAL went back to American Car and Foundry for more of these cars in 1926. Virtually identical to the previous series, they were converted to deluxe cars by the Portsmouth shops in 1936. They were modernized in 1954 with wide, sealed windows and air conditioning. The relative effectiveness of the gray paint scheme can be judged in comparison with the other lightweight cars in the photo. Shown in Jacksonville, Fla. in February of 1969. *(Ron Plazzotta)*

SAL PB 820, series 815-828, class PC9

▼ This coach, from the same series, is shown in the standard green scheme. This car, unlike other cars in the series, was not converted to deluxe seating. As a result, was able to seat 74 people in two compartments. It is shown here in the consist of the GULF WIND, an SAL train that ran from Jacksonville, Fla. out the panhandle of Florida to Chattahoocee, Fla., and on to New Orleans, La. via the L&N. Shown in Tallahassee, Fla. on February 19, 1967. *(George Berisso)*

SAL PB 841, series 840-849

▲ This beautiful coach was originally built for the C&O by Pullman in 1930, and rebuilt in 1948. Never one to turn down a bargain, this series of cars was acquired by the SAL. As a result of the relative "newness" of these cars, they stayed in service up until the advent of Amtrak. These coaches had 54 seats and were 70'9" long. This particular car, former C&O 730, is shown bringing up the rear of a train in Ocala, Fla. in May of 1968.

(Ron Plazzotta)

SAL PB 843, series 840-849

▲ Here is another view of one of the ex-C&O coaches, former 743. Unlike other modernized cars, the windows were not enlarged, but simply sealed, retaining the original window pattern. These older coaches provided a fine ride for the passengers of the secondary trains to which they were assigned. Shown in Atlanta, Ga. in May of 1966. *(Howard Robins)*

SAL PB 850, series 850-859

▼ The second lot of ex-C&O cars was virtually identical to the first, also having been built in 1930 by Pullman. The cars were modernized and air conditioning was added in 1937. This particular car was former C&O 726, and, unlike other cars in the series, had 64 seats. Shown here in Tampa, Fla. in May of 1968. *(Joseph Oates)*

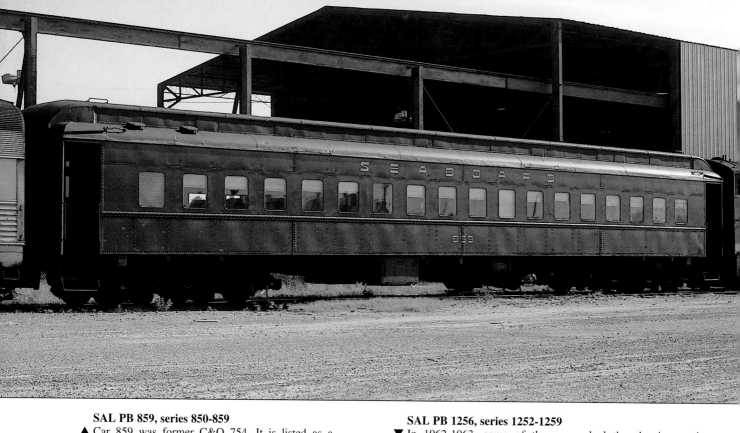

SAL PB 859, series 850-859

▲ Car 859 was former C&O 754. It is listed as a "deluxe coach," having been built by Pullman in 1930 and converted to air conditioning in 1935. This car was capable of handling 45 passengers in two compartments, one of which was a smoking section. It is shown in St. Petersburg, Fla. in June of 1969. *(Paul Coe)*

SAL PB 1256, series 1252-1259

▼ In 1962-1963, some of these cars had the sleeping equipment removed and were converted to coaches. As a result, they lost their names, retaining only their numbers. This car, originally a 10 section 1 drawing room 2 compartment Pullman named *New Lyme*, was built in 1923. Over the years, these cars were gradually retired as passenger service declined and the newer lightweight cars could handle the need. It is shown in Atlanta, Ga. in June of 1964. *(Howard Robins)*

20

SAL PB 833, series 830-835, class PC10

▲ In 1936, the SAL purchased these cars from Pullman Bradley. Built with wide windows, full skirting and air conditioning, these cars were "pre-streamline" cars, being built just prior to the delivery of the first lightweight streamlined cars. These 74'9" cars could seat a total of 76 people in two compartments. Built in Worcester, Mass., these cars were popularized by the on-line New Haven, and were later modeled by American Flyer. Shown in Jacksonville, Fla. in February of 1969. *(Ron Plazzotta)*

SAL PB 6203, series 6200-6207

▲ Among the first lightweight coaches to be purchased by the SAL were these cars, bought from Budd in 1939. Having only a single compartment, they were capable of seating 60 people comfortably. Notice that this car still has the skirting along the underframe. This was later removed to facilitate access to the equipment under the car. Shown in Atlanta, Ga. in 1957. *(Howard Robins)*

SAL PB 6208, series 6208-6214

▼ In 1940, the Seaboard went back to Budd for additional coaches to equip its growing passenger service. These cars had a capacity of 56 people. The sacrifice of four seats was to allow for a larger ladies' lavatory, with a dressing table. The side skirts are gone, typical of the cars' appearance in later years. Notice, too, the RF&P coach following this car. It was built by Pullman, and provides a good comparison of the differences between Pullman and Budd cars. Shown on the former ACL at Lakeland, Fla. in May of 1971. *(Howard Robins)*

SAL PB 6217, series 6215-6226

▲ The intervention of World War II prevented the SAL from ordering such extravagances as lightweight passenger coaches, so it was 1947 before the SAL was able to return to Budd for additional coaches to cover its expanding passenger trade. These cars had still larger lavatory-lounges than the previous cars, reducing the seating capacity to 52 people. This car still retains its side skirting when it was shot in Atlanta, Ga. in March of 1969. *(Howard Robins)*

SAL PB 6229, series 6227-6229

▲ In 1948, the SAL ordered these cars from Budd. Again, seating capacity was reduced to 50 patrons to allow for more amenities, as the luggage shelves and writing desks that these cars featured. These little features, along with more leg room from fewer seats, helped the SAL stay competitive for the long distance Florida traffic. Shown in Tampa, Fla. in February of 1969. *(Ron Plazzotta)*

SAL PB 6233, series 6232-6234

▼ These cars were purchased used from the C&O. Built by Budd in 1948, this car was ex-C&O 1607. Seating only 44 people, this car had a small lounge with capacity of eight passengers and a writing desk. Shown in Atlanta, Ga. in June of 1964, it still retains the distinctive Budd side skirting. *(Howard Robins)*

SAL PB 6237, series 6235-6241

▲ In 1955, the Seaboard purchased these coaches from Pullman. Seating 52 passengers in two sections, these cars had a 10 seat lounge in the center of the car, they were built to plan 7650. Equipped with the latest technologies, such as disk brakes, these cars were definitely the high water mark of SAL coaches. Shown in West Palm Beach, Fla. in March of 1968. *(Paul Coe)*

SAL PB 6242, series 6242-6251

▼ Built by Pullman in 1950 as the C&O 1656 to plan 7600, this car was later acquired by the SAL. The Seaboard simply repainted the top portion of the car gray while keeping the lower fluting. These cars were capable of seating 52 people. Shown in St. Petersburg, Fla. on December of 1967. *(Paul Coe)*

SAL PB 6253, series 6252-6257New

▼ Among the cars acquired in 1965 from the FEC were these coaches, originally built in 1939 by Budd. This particular car was ex-FEC *New Smyrna Beach*. It had the capacity of 60 passengers in a single compartment. Shown in Atlanta, Ga. in May of 1967. *(Howard Robins)*

SAL PB 6267, series 6266-6270

▲ Here is another coach, also built by Pullman in 1950 to plan 7593-A. This car was among those acquired from the FEC and is ex-FEC *Canal Point*. This car had the capacity of 56 people in a single compartment. The SAL put these ex-FEC cars to good use. Shown in Tampa, Fla. in February of 1970.

(Howard Robins)

SAL PB 6269, series 6266-6270

▼ No, your eyes don't deceive you! This is a Seaboard car in IC colors. Among the cars the SAL obtained from the FEC in 1965 were these coaches, painted in IC colors for the CITY OF MIAMI. This particular car is the ex-FEC *Lantana*. Built by Pullman in 1950, it could seat 56 people in its single compartment. Shown in Atlanta, Ga. in May of 1966. *(Howard Robins)*

DINERS

HEAVYWEIGHT DINERS

SAL DA 227, series 226-227, class DC8

▲ This car was built by Pullman in 1925 as the *Lake Wakes*, and modernized by the SAL Portsmouth shops in 1937. The car was 76'4" long, while the dining compartment was 37'7", and could seat 36 people. Note the fresh gladioli adorning the tables through the windows, evidence that the Seaboard still took pride in its dining car service even at this late date. Shown bringing up the rear of the train GULF WIND on February 19, 1967 in Tallahassee, Fla. *(George Berisso)*

SAL DA 240, series 237-242, class DC9

◄ Here is a view of the galley side of the diner. The three small, half height windows are where the kitchen is located. Pullman built this car in 1926, and like the preceding car, was 76'4" long with a 37'7" dining section capable of seating 36 people. Originally named *Lake Lafayette*, this car weighed in at a whopping 83 tons, making it understandable why these cars were called "heavyweights." Shown in Hamlet, N. C. on August 31, 1965.

(George Berisso)

SAL Grill Car 858

▼ Two of the ex-C&O cars, 849 and 858, were converted to grill cars in 1953. The 858, shown here, is ex-C&O 753, while the 849 was ex-C&O 751. As Grill cars, they could seat 15 people in booths or at the counter. There was a passenger compartment capable of seating 18 people. A popular assignment for these cars was on trains 9 and 10, the PALMLAND, which was essentially a long distance local. This car is shown from the aisle side and is in Chicago, Ill. in July of 1969. *(Paul Coe)*

SAL Grill Car 858

▶ Here is an interior shot of car 858, showing the grill area. Behind the grill area is a small pantry. The grill itself is the area along the wall opposite the counter. As a result of this modification, the window arrangement was noticeably different from one side of the car to the other. Grill cars were the railroad's answer to providing food service on marginal trains without the expense of a dining car. Shown in Chicago, Ill. in July of 1969. *(Paul Coe)*

26

SAL DA 1007,
series 1004-1007, class DC6
▼ Built by Pullman in 1922, this car was air conditioned in 1936 and modernized by the Portsmouth shops in 1937. It was capable of seating 36 people, but with extended 48" tables on both sides, it could seat up to 48 people. It was 76'4" long, and was sometimes used as a lounge car. Retired as their duties on long distance trains were assumed by lightweight equipment, by 1966 there were only five heavyweight diners on the roster. This car, shot in Atlanta, Ga. in January of that year, had already been stricken from the roster. Thankfully, the Atlanta Chapter, NRHS, preserved it. *(Howard Robins)*

DINERS

LIGHTWEIGHT DINERS

SAL DA 6112, series 6106-6114

▲ Built by Budd in 1947, this car represents the high water mark of Seaboard dining cars. It was capable of seating 48 patrons in half of its length, while the remainder of the car supported the kitchen and pantry. As expected, these cars served on the premier trains. It is a good bet that this car is in town with the SILVER COMET as it was photographed in Atlanta, Ga. in 1957. *(Howard Robins)*

SAL DA 6119, series 6119-6120

▲ Built by Pullman in 1950 for the FEC as the *Fort Ribault*, this car was sold to the Seaboard in 1965 and renumbered 6119. It was capable of seating 36 people in its dining section. Most long distance trains carried two diners, one for the Pullman passengers and another for the coach passengers. Shown in Jacksonville, Fla. in June of 1968. *(Howard Robins)*

SAL DA 6120, series 6119-6120

▶ Here is an interior shot of the former FEC diner *Fort Drum*. Notice the fine crystal water pitchers and vases with fresh flowers on each table. There is nothing lacking or shabby about this service, which would rival that of a fine restaurant. The SAL was known for its fine dining service, a tradition that apparently continued into the SCL era as shown here. Shown in St. Petersburg, Fla. in December of 1968. *(Paul Coe)*

SAL PBO 6400, series 6400-6402

▲ Purchased from Budd in 1939, these cars were the original observation cars for the SILVER METEOR. This particular car was extensively rebuilt in 1943 to the flat end configuration shown to allow use in the middle of the train. It had the capacity of 48 people in the coach section and 24 people in the observation section. This car is shown on a Gainesville Midland steam excursion with 750 sponsored by the Atlanta Chapter, NRHS at Gainesville, Ga. on December 2, 1966. *(Howard Robins)*

28

SAL PBO 6401, series 6400-6402

▶ The other two cars in the series were not rebuilt, but they had diaphragms fitted to their ends, as shown here. Again, this was to facilitate their use in the middle of trains as coach lounge cars. A favorite assignment of the three cars in this series in later years was the SILVER STAR, where they made an unusual sight toward the front of the train just after the head end sleepers. Shown in Gainesville, Ga. in June of 1966.

(Howard Robins)

SAL PBO 6402, series 6400-6402

◀ Here is the last car in the series, shown in its original state without a diaphragm, on the rear of the northbound SILVER STAR at Alexandria, Va. After the delivery of the 6600 series boat tailed observations in 1947, these cars were assigned to other trains. While not dated, this slide was apparently shot sometime in the late 1940's, as evidenced by the heavyweight Pullmans near the head end of the train. It was not until 1949 that the SAL was finally able to take delivery on lightweight sleepers from a backlogged Pullman Company.

(S. Bogen)

SAL PO 6605, series 6600-6605

▲ Built by Budd in 1947, this car is shown on the road's flagship train, the SILVER METEOR. Notice the lack of an end diaphragm and the presence of a drumhead. The three cars assigned to the SILVER METEOR retained this appearance, through the SCL merger and Amtrak, showing the pride the SAL and its successors had in the appearance of its flagship train. The other three cars, 6600, 6603 and 6604, had diaphragms installed on the rear for mid-train operation. This car is shown in the PRR at the northern end of its run in Sunnyside Yard, New York, N. Y. on March 14, 1965. *(Matt Herson)*

SAL PO 6602, series 6600-6605

▼ Here is an interior shot showing the lounge and bar section of the interior. Capable of seating 34 patrons in the lounge and 24 patrons in the observation section, these cars served as the bar for the premier trains. What a delight it must have been to enjoy an "Orange Blossom Special" cocktail in the observation section while watching the cold north recede behind you. Shown in Winter Haven, Fla. in December of 1969.

(Paul Coe)

29

SLEEPERS

HEAVYWEIGHT SLEEPERS

SAL PS *Weepers Tower*, 1235, series 1231-1235

▲ At the breakup of the Pullman Company in 1948, the SAL obtained a group of heavyweight Pullmans as part of the settlement. This car was a 8 Section 1 Drawing Room 3 Double Bedroom Pullman originally named *Point Yorke* that was part of a nine car series built in 1923. The two-tone gray paint scheme was the last paint scheme used by Pullman on the cars. The "Pullman" name was simply replaced by an 8" high silver Seaboard name. This car was converted to a coach after this photo was taken. Shown in Atlanta, Ga. in July of 1963. *(Howard Robins)*

SAL PS *Lake Chicot*, 1252, series 1252-1259

▼ Initially, the cars obtained from Pullman were retained as sleeping cars. For the most part, these cars had been assigned to the SAL before ownership had been transferred, running on the premier trains prior to the delivery of the lightweight sleepers. This car, also an 8-1-3 Pullman like the previous car, is shown from the opposite side. Surprisingly, the 1966 roster still lists five heavyweight cars still in service as sleeping cars. Shown in Atlanta, Ga. in October of 1964. *(Howard Robins)*

SAL PS 16 *Stone Mountain*, series 15-17
▲ In 1949, the SAL went to American Car and Foundry for three 6 Double Bedroom-Buffet-Lounge cars. Equipped with a 21' lounge section and a bar, these cars where ordered for service on the SILVER COMET, as reflected by their names, *Red Mountain, Stone Mountain*, and *Kennesaw Mountain*, all geographic features on the Altanta-Birmingham run of the train. This car is shown in Atlanta, Ga. in May of 1967. *(Howard Robins)*

SAL PS 19, *Palm Beach*, series 18-20
▼ In 1956, the SAL found itself in need of upgrading the SILVER METEOR to reflect the changing needs of its patronage. The SAL wanted to add dome cars, to attract vacationers, but was prevented from doing so by the low clearances in the tunnel just south of the Washington, D. C. Union Station. The solution from Pullman was these three cars, with large glass panels flat in the roof, built to plan 4202, and called Sun Lounges. Shown in the consist of the SILVER METEOR at Sunnyside Yard on the PRR in New York, N. Y. on March 15, 1965. *(Matt Herson)*

31

SAL PS 20, *Hollywood Beach*, series 18-20

▲ Here is an interior shot of the sun lounge cars, showing the glass windows and the lounge section. There was a lot of heat gain from the Florida sun, so the overhead windows had shades that were drawn until air conditioning could cool off the car. The three cars, *Miami Beach*, *Palm Beach,* and *Hollywood Beach*, were 5 Double Bed Room-Bar-Lounge cars with a seating capacity of 21 people in the lounge. Spending their entire service lives on the SILVER METEOR these cars served as lounges for the first class Pullman passengers at the front of the train. Shown enroute near Winter Haven, Fla. in October of 1970. *(Paul Coe)*

SAL PS 25, *Richmond*, series 25-37

▼ This is the first car in a series of thirteen 10 roomette, 6 double bedroom sleeping cars built by Pullman in 1949 to plan 4140-A. Shown in Tampa, Fla. on May 1, 1971, this is the last sleeper to Venice, Fla. Amtrak discontinued this service when it took over the SCL's passenger service. For years, this run was famous to railfans because it used doodlebug 2028 for power. *(Howard Robins)*

SAL PS 29, *Raleigh*, series 25-37

▲ Like many other railroads, the SAL named its sleepers for cities or geographic features along the line. It was this series of cars that finally eliminated heavyweight sleepers from the SILVER METEOR and the SILVER STAR, making them totally lightweight trains. This car was later destroyed in a wreck. Shown at an unknown location in May of 1969. *(Dr. Art Peterson)*

SAL PS 36, *Atlanta*, series 25-37

▼ Here is a shot of one of the 10 - 6 sleepers from the bedroom side. Of particular note here is the fluted roof, unusual for a Pullman built car. Fastidious about the appearance of its stellar passenger trains, the SAL insisted that Pullman supply the cars with fluted roofs. Pullman did not know how to weld the fluting to the curved roof surfaces like Budd did, resulting in the roof panels buckling. While the problem was finally solved, it appears that age may be causing a reoccurrence on this car. Shown on October 1, 1967 in Chicago, Ill. *(Owen Leander, R.J. Yanosey Collection)*

34

SAL PS 43, *Miami,* **series 38-43**

▲ The SAL did go to Budd for six 10 - 6 sleepers, as the one shown here, in 1949. The breakup of the Pullman Company's monopoly on railroad sleeping cars allowed other builders to build sleeping cars. Shown in St. Petersburg, Fla. in October of 1968. *(Paul Coe)*

SAL PS 50, *Bay Pines,* **series 50-55**

▼ Built by Budd in 1955, these cars had 5 bedrooms, 1 compartment, 4 roomettes, and 4 sections. They were state of the art for the time, having disc brakes. This is the room side of the car. Shown in St. Petersburg, Fla. in April of 1968. *(Paul Coe)*

SAL PS 55, *Cedartown*, series 50-55
▲ Named for smaller cities on the line, the 5-4-4-1 sleepers still got prestigious assignments, as the SILVER METEOR. Here is the *Cedartown*, the last car in the series, from the aisle side. Shown in Auburndale, Fla. in January of 1971, on the SCL train SOUTH WIND. *(Paul Coe)*

SAL PS 60, *Boca Grande*, series 60-62
▼ Built by Pullman in 1956 to plan 4201, these cars were among the last passenger cars purchased new by the SAL. This is a 5 double bedroom, 2 compartment, 2 drawing room car. While these cars were named for resort cities in Florida, this car is shown far from home on PRR train #14 in Union Station in Columbus, Ohio on December 1, 1962. *(Paul C. Winters)*

35

SAL PS 71, *Venice*, series 70-75

▲ In mid 1956, the Seaboard purchased these cars from Pullman in an effort to boost sagging ridership of long distance trains. The idea of this car, an 11 double bed room sleeper built to plan 4198A, was to provide afford-able accommodations for traveling families. This car is shown in Chicago, Ill. in September of 1968, after the SCL merger.

(Owen Leander, R.J. Yanosey Collection)

SAL PS 71, *Venice*, series 70-75

▲ Here is another shot of the sleeper *Venice*, this time from the aisle side. Like any other sleeper, the window arrangement varies from one side to the other, a result of the car's function. These cars were usually assigned to the SILVER METEOR. Shown in Sebring, Fla. *(Warren Calloway collection)*

SAL PS 74, *Avon Park*, series 70-75

▼ This car, another 11 double bed room sleeper, is the next to the last car in the series. This car is shown at West Lake Wales, Fla. in February of 1968 in the SILVER METEOR. *(Paul Coe)*

SAL XM 14754, series 14159-14958

▲ Our first boxcar is this car, rebuilt in 1952. The original cars were obsolete outside braced, wood sided boxcars nearing the end of their service lives. They came from the series numbered from 15000-16999, and were built in 1930. The result was a steel sheathed car with a fishbelly underframe that looked, for all intents and purposes, like the B6 class of boxcars. This car is shown in the classic *Route of the Orange Blossom Special* paint scheme at Tampa, Fla. in February 1965.

(Howard Robins)

SAL XM 14900, series 14159-14958

◄ The SAL apparently thought a lot of their re-built boxcars, for they traveled all over the country in interchange service. This particular car is shown here at Lawrence, Kan. in October of 1955, only a few years after rebuilding. These cars were probably the last cars painted in the *Orange Blossom Special* paint scheme. *(Don Ball collection)*

SAL XM 14100, series 14000-14158; 14959-14999

▼ While most of the cars from the 14000 series had six foot doors, the SAL rebuilt this group of 200 cars with eight foot doors in 1954, giving them a somewhat unusual appearance. They had a rated capacity of 50 tons. The inset along the bottom of the sides bear testimony of the car's previous life as a single sheathed, wood sided boxcar. Shown at Tallahassee, Fla. in May of 1976. *(George Eichelberger)*

SAL XM 14117, series 14000-14158; 14959-14999

▲ Despite their low inside height of 8'6", these cars proved to be useful, and many continued in maintenance service, virtually unaltered, after being retired from revenue service. This car sports the *Route of the Silver Meteor* paint scheme with the 56" herald. Shown in Wildwood, Fla., on September 16, 1973.

(August Staebler, Stan Jackowski collection)

38

SAL XM 17161, series 17000-17699, class B6

▼ In 1934, the Seaboard went to builder Pullman-Standard to purchase 700 40-foot single sheathed steel boxcars of 50 ton capacity. These cars had 6' doors and were 8'9" high inside. Very similar to the PRR class X-29 boxcars, these cars were actually the ARA 1932 design boxcar. The SAL liked these cars enough that it went back to Pullman for another 300, numbered 17700-17999, before year's end. Shown here at Bartow, Fla. in February 1975. *(George Eichelberger)*

SAL XM 18198, series 18000-18999, class B6
▲ The B6 class boxcars were very enduring, lasting their owner, and subsequent owners, well into the 1980's. These cars were built in 1937 by Pullman-Standard, and are identical to the previous series. This particular car is shown with the *Route of the Silver Meteor* paint scheme that the railroad used to advertise its premier train. Shown in Perry, Fla. on May 24, 1974.
(Stan Jackowski, George Eichelberger collection)

SAL XM 18229, series 18000-18999, class B6
▼ The B6 boxcars proved to be very useful, performing in a variety of services. Toward the end of their careers, the railroad found them useful cars for "dirty" types of service, where the only thing that counted was an available car. A surprising number of these cars were in assigned service for such things as hide loading, salt loading, fish-meal loading, fertilizer and sludge service. Shown here at Trilby, Fla. in February of 1975.
(Greg Michels, George Eichelberger collection)

39

SAL XM 18923, series 18000-18999, class B6

▲ Other members of the B6 class were still assigned to merchandise loading, while the remainder were in the general pool. As these cars reached the ends of their useful lives, a number of them were rebuilt into all kinds of maintenance of way cars. All totaled, the Seaboard had 2700 cars of this, or a very similar design. Shown at Hamlet, N. C. on June 1, 1974. (*Larry Goolsby*)

SAL XM 19046, series 19000-19499, class B7

▼ In what appears to be another copy of a PRR boxcar design, the Seaboard purchased 500 of these "round roof" cars with single 6' doors from by Pullman-Standard in 1941. While these cars were pioneered by the PRR as their X31 class boxcars, they were adopted by the ARA in 1937, and used by other roads as well. For their time, their increased interior height of 10' (versus 8'9") made them the first "high cube" cars. Sporting the last boxcar scheme, this car is shown in Tampa, Fla. on an unknown date. (*George Eicheberger*)

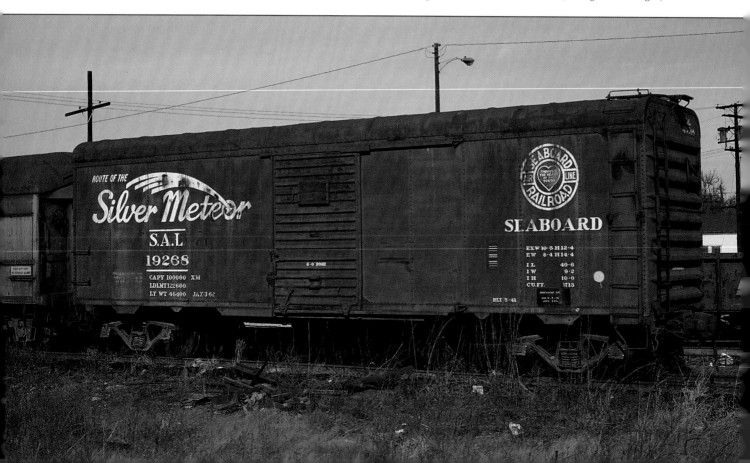

SAL XM 19268, series 19000-19499, class B7

▲ As time passed, some of these cars also ended their careers in maintenance of way service, as this car shown here. The paint scheme on this car dates from 1944, and is the original paint scheme. Note the 40" herald with the 6" name underneath. This car is shown in Atlanta, Ga. in April of 1979.

(Lon Coone, Warren Calloway collection)

SAL XM 19838, series 19700-19999, class B9

▼ In 1944, the SAL, in dire need of new boxcars to ease the burden on its aging fleet, went to the War Production Board for additional cars. The answer was the class B8, based on the 1937 ARA design, ordered from Pullman-Standard, delivered late that year, and numbered from 19500-19699. In 1945, additional cars were ordered creating the series shown here. These 50 ton cars had 6' doors and an interior height of 10'. Like the previous classes, these cars did yeoman service, and were often assigned "dirty" loads. This car, shown in the 1963 billboard scheme, is at Hopewell, Va. in April of 1966. *(Dr. Art Peterson)*

SAL XM 20068, series 20000-20199

◀ Encouraged by the success of its 1952 box-car rebuilding program, the SAL decided to rebuild wooden boxcars from 15000-15999 and 16000-16999 series into these cars at its West Jacksonville shops in 1955. These cars were fitted with steel sides and 8 foot, staggered doors. Nearly new 20068 is shown at Lawrence, Kan. in November of 1955.

(Don Ball collection)

SAL XM 20102, series 20000-20199

▲ These cars, with their larger 8" doors, proved very useful in general freight service throughout their careers. Several of these cars survived into the 1980's in maintenance or company stores service. The fishbelly under-frame and inset fascia along the bottom of the sides give away the fact that the car has been rebuilt. This car is shown at an Talbotton, Ga. on April 3, 1975, still in its original paint scheme. *(Larry Goolsby)*

SAL XM 20145, series 20000-20199

◄ Another shot of a nearly new rebuilt boxcar, again shown in Lawrence, Kan. in November of 1955. For some reason, the SAL decided to experiment with a few members of this series. While this car is not one of them, eight of these cars were rebuilt in 1955 with roof hatches, becoming the first LC type cars the SAL had. The larger 8' door opening allowed more leakage of powder, resulting in subsequent roof hatch boxcars having 6' doors. *(Don Ball collection)*

SAL XM 21776, series 21700-21999

▼ In 1959, the Seaboard went to Magor Car of Clifton, N. J. for what would be the its last 40 foot boxcars. These cars were 50 ton cars equipped with nailable steel floors, roller bearing trucks, lading anchors and 10' doors. The cars spent most of their careers in assigned service moving appliances from northern factories to southern distribution centers. This car was assigned to Westinghouse in Columbus, Ohio, and is shown at Woodland, Ga. on March 24, 1973 in its original paint scheme.

(Larry Goolsby)

SAL XM 21798, series 21700-21999

▲ A fair number of these cars were repainted during their service lives. 21798 has the 1963 billboard scheme, and shows evidence of having its door replaced. These cars proved to be very useful in all types of merchandise traffic where larger doors were needed. Shown at Spooner, Wis. on August 25, 1974. (*Ron Plazzotta*)

SAL XM 24136, series 24000-24499, class B10

▲ After the war ended, the SAL had only three types of single door steel cars and a number of composite sided cars. Most of the latter were no longer suitable for the expanding requirements of post-war traffic. By now, Pullman-Standard had perfected their famous PS-1 boxcar, so the SAL ordered its first 500 of these cars, with 8' seven panel Superior doors, in 1948. Shown here in 1964 billboard scheme at Hamlet, N. C. on January 19, 1985. (*Paul Faulk*)

SAL XM 24359, series 24000-24499, class B10

▼ The PS-1 boxcars, like most of the other 40' boxcars on the SAL, were of 50 ton capacity. The slogan, *Route of the Silver Comet* is the delivery paint scheme. The utilitarian PS-1s quickly became the standard steel boxcar for the SAL, and were assigned to all types of service. Shown here at Live Oak, Fla. in July of 1969. (*Howard Robins*)

SAL XM 24452, series 24000-24499, class B10

▲ The Seaboard modified a number of the PS-1s with various fixtures, as insulation, vents and load restraints, assigned them to special service, and gave them special paint schemes. Shown here in Richmond, Va. in April of 1971, this car sports the gray version of the *Route of the Silver Comet* paint scheme, indicative of its vents for handling paper pulp from Bowater Paper in Catawba, S. C. *(Dr. Art Peterson)*

SAL XM 24579, series 24500-24999

▼ The first order of PS-1s was a success, for in 1951, the Seaboard went back to Pullman-Standard for another 500 cars. These cars were identical to the first order, but were delivered with 8' corrugated Youngstown doors instead of the Superior paneled doors. These cars survived long enough to be rebuilt into SCL class X-7-c series 11800-12290. This car is shown with the 1963 billboard lettering scheme at Jennings, Fla. in March 1970. *(Howard Robins)*

44

SAL XM 24754, series 24500-24999

▲ This is another PS-1, shown here with the 1964 Railroad Roman billboard lettering. Most of these cars seemed to end up in this paint scheme, probably because these cars were just old enough to need repainting by the merger, and that was the current scheme. At any rate, this scheme looked good on these cars. Shown east of Bartow, Fla. in May of 1970. *(George Eichelberger)*

SAL XM 24942, series 24500-24999

▼ The *Route of the Silver Comet* paint scheme, shown here, was the delivery paint scheme. Like the billboard scheme, this scheme is a very common style. This scheme features a 40" herald with the 6" name underneath. Shown in Atlanta, Ga. in September of 1970. *(Howard Robins)*

SAL XMI 25099,
series 25000-25499

▶ This particular car was modified with an insulated roof and was assigned at one time to handle beer out of Hillsboro, Fla. While beer does not have to be refrigerated, it is sensitive to extreme variations in temperature, which explains the modification and the paint scheme. The SAL also used the insulated boxcars of the Fruit Growers Express to handle this traffic. This particular car was built in 1952 as part of the last order of PS-1 boxcars from Pullman-Standard. Shown in Winter Haven, Fla. in February of 1974.

(George Eichelberger)

SAL XMI 25255, series 25000-25499

▲ Another beer car again assigned to Tampa, Fla., showing a different paint scheme. Cars with roof insulation used the silver version of the standard scheme, while vented cars and other specialized cars used the gray version. The silver paint was chosen for insulated cars to aid with heat reflection. Shown in Rome, Ga. in June of 1966. (*Bill Folsom*)

SAL XMI 25303, series 25000-25499

▼ This version of the beer car paint scheme was the last version. This particular car was assigned for loading in Tampa, Fla. The beer cars were identical to the other cars of this series, except for cubic capacity, which was 3,743 cu. ft. instead of 3,878 cu. ft., due to 6 inches of insulation in the roof. Shown in Atlanta, Ga. in September of 1970. (*Howard Robins*)

SAL XMI 25403, series 25000-25499

▲ This is the silver version of the original paint scheme for these cars. As such, it is a very attractive car, and it sports the least common variation of the least common slogan. Again, this is another beer car with roof insulation. Of the total of 500 cars, 47 had roof insulation for beer service, and another 35 had Evans DF-2 loaders for appliance service. Shown here at Rome, Ga. in November of 1965. *(Bill Folsom)*

SAL XM 25450, series 25000-25499

▼ This is the red version of the *Route of the Silver Star* paint scheme. While other cars may have sported this slogan, this is the only series of which records can be found. This car is equipped with an 8' Youngstown door and has equipment identical to previous orders of PS-1s. This was likely the delivery paint scheme for these versatile 50 ton cars built in 1952. Shown in Florence, S. C. in April 1970. *(Chuck Yungkurth, Rail Data Services)*

47

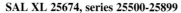

SAL XL 25674, series 25500-25899

▲ This car is one of 23 cars equipped with Spartan Tri Belt loaders, as identified by the unique paint scheme. Another 53 cars were equipped with Evans DF-2 loaders. Both cars had doorway members to eliminate cargo shifting in the door areas, which was a common source of lading damage. Like most of the other cars the SAL modified, the numbers were chosen from the regular series randomly. This car was assigned to Kelvinator in Manitowac, Wis. for appliance loading. Shown in Tampa, Fla. in January of 1975. *(George Eichelberger)*

SAL XL 25775, series 25500-25899

▼ This was the last series 40 foot of PS-1 boxcars purchased from Pullman-Standard by the SAL in 1955. These cars had 8 foot Superior 6 panel doors and were rated at 50 tons. Unlike the previous car, the majority of the cars in this series were in general service. The 40 foot PS-1 with 8 foot doors proved to be a very successful design for the SAL, so successful that successor SCL continued to order them. Shown east of Bartow, Fla. in May of 1970. *(George Eichelberger)*

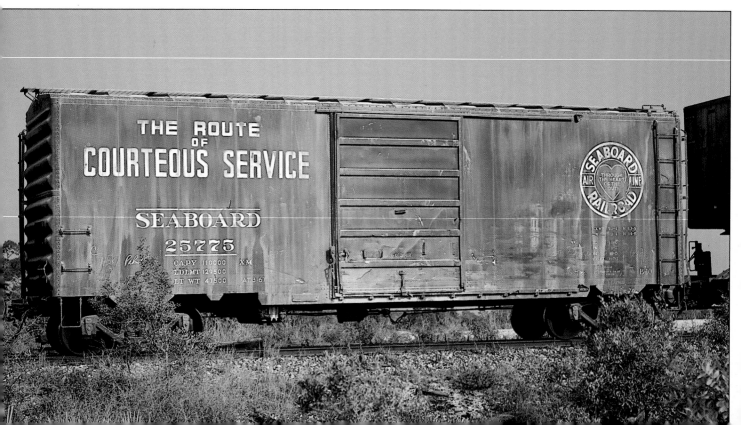

**SAL XM 11041,
series 11000-11699, class AF1**

▶ The Seaboard, like many other railroads, had a fleet of double door boxcars originally designed for automobile and furniture traffic, hence the classification "AF." These cars quickly found their way into all types of service where their large door openings were an advantage. They lasted well after the SAL disappeared from the railroad scene. Shown here on the NYSW at Little Ferry, N. J. on November 5, 1967. *(George Berisso)*

BOXCARS

40' DOUBLE DOOR BOXCARS

SAL XM 11353, 11248 series 11000-11699, class AF1

▲ Built in 1940 by Pullman-Standard as a 40' car with a capacity of 50 tons and a 12'6" door opening, these cars were based on the same basic "round roof" design made popular by the PRR. This shot illustrates the reversed version of the *Route of the Silver Meteor* paint scheme. Shown here on the C&O at Parsons Yard in Columbus, Ohio in June of 1962. *(Paul C. Winters)*

SAL XM 11790, series 11700-11999, class AF2

▼ To say that the round roof cars were popular would be an understatement, for the Seaboard was apparently impressed enough with the previous series of 700 cars purchased in 1940 that the went back to Pullman-Standard in 1942 for another 300 of these cars. These cars are virtually identical to the previous series, except they are an inch shorter inside and 400 pounds heavier. Shown here in Columbus Ohio in February of 1968. *(Paul C. Winters)*

SAL XM 11912, series 11700-11999, class AF2

▲ The paint scheme shown here, with 1963 billboard lettering. These cars performed all kinds of service, which took them all over the country. As a result of the lack of auto traffic during the war, railroads like the SAL dis-covered these cars were very useful in handling lumber that was needed by the effort. Shown here in Columbus, Ohio in August of 1969.

(Paul C. Winters)

SAL XM 20053

▶ The Seaboard decided to equip one car of the 20000 series with 20' double doors to handle lumber and canstock loading. This was accomplished by fitting two 10' doors on each side, offset so that the entire inte-rior of the car was exposed. This required the under-frame be beefed up to com-pensate for the large open-ings in the sides. The car apparently met with suc-cess, as similar cars fol-lowed. This car is shown in the scrap line at Uceta Yard in Tampa, Fla. on December 1, 1973.

(Stan Jackowski, George Eichelberger collection)

SAL XM 20202, series 20200-20209

◀ The design changes made from what was learned from the 20053 resulted in some noticeable differences in this series of cars, rebuilt by the West Jacksonville shops in 1957. These changes are increased height (from 8'7" to 10'5"), corrugated ends, and fishbelly fascia pan-els for support along the bottom of the sides. These changes completely obliter-ated the cars' heritage as single sheathed boxcars with 6' doors. While built for lumber, at least one of these cars was assigned to paper loading, where its wide doors would have served it well. This par-ticular car is shown in Grandview Yard, on the PRR, in Columbus, Ohio on April 21, 1963. *(Paul C. Winters)*

SAL XM 22007, series 22000-22199, class AF2
▲ Identical to the previous series of class AF2 boxcars, and virtually identical to the class AF1 boxcars, this series, built in 1942 by Pullman-Standard, represents another 200 cars of this useful class. All totaled, the SAL had 1200 of these double-door, 40' round roof cars. The only explanation for the disjointed series is that the SAL had cars occupying the 12000 series when these cars were purchased. This very enduring car is shown at Ocala, Fla. on December 24, 1982. *(George Eichelberger)*

**SAL XM 22297,
series 22200-22449, class AF3**
▶ The SAL went back to Pullman-Standard in 1945 to purchase these 50 ton cars, based on a pre-war design, with 12' 6" door openings, and an intermediate height of 10'3. The use of offset doors on a 40' car provided better access to the interior, and created solid wall space opposite the door which reduced cargo shifting. Shown in maintenance of way service at Ocala, Fla. in April of 1973.
(George Eichelberger)

SAL XM 22458, series 22450-22949, class AF4
▼ In 1948, the SAL was back at Pullman-Standard to order these cars, with a capacity of 50 tons, but with the interior height of 10'6" that quickly became standard after the war and a door opening of 14'. This heavily "touched-up" car is shown as it passes through Columbus, Ohio in July of 1968. These cars saw a variety of uses other than just lumber, including paper service and service to Maxwell House Coffee in Jacksonville, Fla. *(Paul C. Winters)*

SAL XM 22697, series 22450-22929, class AF4

▲ This particular car shows the *Route of Courteous Service* paint scheme that was the delivery scheme. Note the railroad name is spelled out, rather than using the initials, and that the herald and slogans are "reversed" from their normal positions to compensate for the offset doors. The cars were delivered with two pairs of 7', seven panel Superior doors. This car is shown at Baldwin, Fla. on April 20, 1973.

(George Eichelberger, Joseph Oates collection)

52

SAL XM 23307, series 23000-23499, class AF5

▼ In 1948, the SAL went to Pressed Steel for 500 of these 50 ton cars with 14' door openings. Having the now standard height of 10'6", these cars differed from the Pullman cars by having Youngstown corrugated doors and, of course, different ends. This car is shown in the *Route of the Silver Meteor* paint scheme as it sits in St. Mary's Ga. on April 15, 1972, where it was likely sent for loading at the large Gilman Paper plant there. *(Bill Folsom)*

BOXCARS

50' SINGLE DOOR BOXCARS

SAL XML 15052, series 15000-15199

▲ With the 15000 series vacant, the SAL was free to assign this series of numbers to some brand new, state of the art Pullman-Standard PS-1 boxcars built in 1962. These cars were equipped with 10' doors, Evans DF-2 load devices and 30" Pullman Hydroframe 60 cushioned underframes. They stood 10'6" tall inside and had a capacity of 70 tons. Shown in Columbus, Ohio in Parsons Yard on the C&O in July of 1962. *(Paul C. Winters)*

SAL XML 15242, series 15200-15499

▼ Painted in this green scheme to call attention to their specialized equipment, these cars, and the previous series to which they are identical, were the first of what crews referred to as the "Green Hornets." The color of the doors is due to the fact that they were aluminum, rather than painted. With good equipment, these cars spent a fair amount of time off line. Shown here on the DT&I at Schafer Junction in Dearborn, Mich. in October of 1963. *(Emery Gulash)*

 53

SAL XML 15292, series 15200-15499

▲ As one might expect with their specialized equipment, the "Green Hornets" tended to be in assigned service for paper traffic, which utilized the specialized equipment to good advantage. A number of these cars were also in merchandise service. Over time, the 10' aluminum doors did not fare well against the ravages of service and fork lift drivers, so they were consequently replaced with regular steel Youngstown doors. Photos of cars with aluminum doors are rather rare as a result. This nearly new car is shown in Atlanta, Ga. in March of 1963, shortly after it was built.

(Howard Robins)

SAL XML 16028, series 16000-16299.

◄ This nice shot of 16028 was taken in April of 1962 when the car was brand new at the Pullman-Standard plant at Bessemer, Ala. Rated at 70 tons, and dimensionally identical to the 15000 series, the principal difference between the cars appears to be the cushion underframe size and type. The 15000 series had 30" cushioning devices, while the 16000 series had 20" cushioning devices.

(Pullman-Standard, Jim Kinkaid collection)

SAL XML 16173, series 16000-16299

▼ Here is a shot of one of these cars in service, probably moving a load of paper products. Door type on these cars appears to have varied, as Superior, Youngstown and Pullman are all listed as door types on these cars. The door opening was 10' wide. This car is shown at the famous Tower 55 in Fort Worth, Tex. in October of 1962, just six months after leaving Bessemer.

(K. B. King, Richard Yaremko collection)

SAL XML 16568, series 16550-16749

▲ The year 1965 brought a new type of "Green Hornet" and a new variation of the paint scheme, adopted in late 1964. The style of the lettering was changed from block to Railroad Roman. These 75 ton cars, built by American Car and Foundry, were 10'6" high inside, had a single Youngstown 10' plug door and a 20" Keystone cushioned underframe. Shown in Atlanta, Ga., on October 28, 1983. *(George Eichelberger)*

SAL XML 16622, series 16550-16749

▲ When new, the "Green Hornets" were certainly eye catching cars, as evidenced by the number of slides taken of them around that time period. This car is certainly no exception, as it rolls through Chamblee, Ga. in January of 1966. Equipped with smooth interiors and Evans DF-2 load retraining devices, these 75 ton cars were very useful to their owner handling kraft paper traffic, and eliminating damage to the large rolls. *(Bill Folsom)*

SAL XML 16659, series 16550-16749

▼ Showing how the paint faded over the years, here is one of the American Car and Foundry plug door boxcars in the snow. The plug door, associated with refrigerator and insulated cars, was advantageous in kraft paper service because it provided a continuously smooth interior. The need for door bracing to keep cargo from being damaged by falling into the door offsets was eliminated. Shown in Greensboro, N. C. on the Southern on February 19, 1979. *(Bob Graham)*

SAL XM 21002, series 21000-21699

▲ In 1959, the Seaboard, following the trend to larger freight cars and bolstered by the success of the 40' PS-1 boxcar, went to Pullman-Standard for 700 standard PS-1 boxcars with 10' doors, nailable steel floors and roller bearing trucks. These cars were equipped with Evans DF-2 loaders to reduce freight damage, had a capacity of 50 tons and were the standard 10'6" high inside. This car is shown at Viola, Del. on August 4, 1977. *(George Berisso)*

SAL XM 21438, series 21000-21699

▼ The 1964 billboard lettering shown on this car seems to be the most popular paint scheme for this series. In the early 1960's the SAL decided to equip two groups of four cars each with cushioning devices as an experiment. 21605-21609 were equipped with a Freightmaster 10" cushioning device, while 21600-21604 were equipped with a 24" cushioned underframes. The experiment was a success, and these cars became the predecessors for the first "Green Hornet" boxcars. Shown in Atlanta, Ga. in February, 1977. *(Howard Robins)*

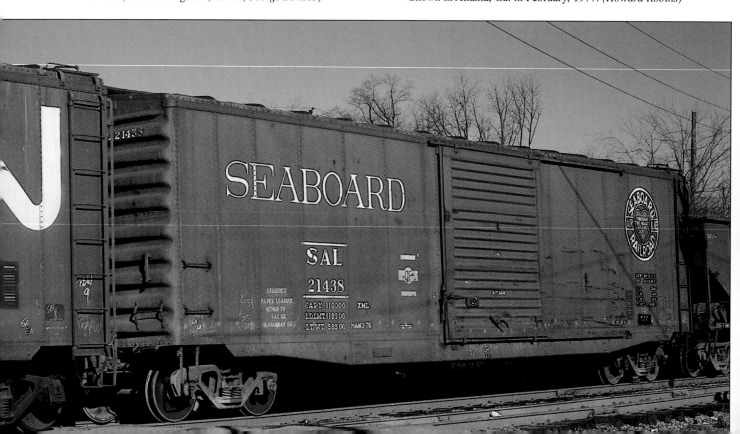

SAL XM 21496, series 21000-21699

▲ When delivered, these cars were painted in the *Route of Courteous Service* scheme shown here. By all accounts, this was no idle boast for the SAL. It was a way of life for them. These cars enjoyed a long service life, becoming the standard 50' boxcar for the SAL. They handled a variety of freight, including chemicals, paper, wire, textiles and merchandise. Shown at Winter Haven Fla. on April 12, 1974. *(George Eichelberger)*

SAL XM 21642, series 21000-21699

▼ On the last 95 cars in the series, the Seaboard decided to use Spartan Tri-Belt load restraining devices instead of the Evans DF-2 restraints. The only visible evidence of this difference from the outside of these cars was the large, Tri-Belt logo, which replaced the slogan. This car is shown in Raleigh, N. C. in December of 1974.

(George Eichelberger)

SAL XM 26734, series 26000-26999

▲ Built by Pullman-Standard in 1956, this car is a 50' PS-1, equipped with 10' Superior paneled doors, friction bearing trucks and rigid underframes. They were rated for 50 tons and had the cubic capacity of 4,834 cu. ft. The last 25 in the series, 26975-26999, had Spartan Tri-belt loading devices installed, resulting in a modified paint scheme with the Spartan Tri-Belt logo. The wide door openings made the cars of this series very useful for all types of service. Shown in Reading, Pa. on October 24, 1970. *(Craig Bossler)*

SAL XM 27190, series 27000-27499

▼ In 1955, the Seaboard ordered 500 50-foot boxcars with nine-foot doors from builder American Car and Foundry in St. Louis, Mo. The industry was moving toward larger doors, and the SAL saw the utility of that, for these were the only 50' single door boxcars that did not have ten-foot doors. Still, with a capacity of 50 tons and 4,831 cu. ft., these cars proved useful. Shown on December 7, 1974 in Reading, Pa. *(Craig Bossler)*

SAL XM 27270, series 27000-27499

▲ While this is another American Car and Foundry 50-foot boxcar, the paint scheme is certainly unique. Painted as an experiment, it apparently was not successful, for it appears to have been the only car so done. The large billboard lettering is based on the passenger and locomotive lettering.

Had the experiment been successful, the Seaboard would have had a memorable boxcar paint scheme! Evidence suggests the car was painted in May of 1967, on the eve of the SCL merger. Shown in Manchester, Ga. on November 29, 1974. *(Larry Goolsby)*

SAL XM 27311, series 27000-27499

▲ Here is a shot of the "B" end of one of the American Car and Foundry cars. Note the 4-3-1 Dreadnaught end typical of this design. Pictures suggest that this lettering scheme was the predominant style on these cars in the mid 1960s. Shown on the IHB in LaGrange, Ill. in November of 1974.

(George Eichelberger)

SAL XM 27380, series 27000-27499

▼ Our final shot of the American Car and Foundry 50-foot boxcar shows the 1963 billboard lettering. Though not shown here, these cars were delivered in the *Route of Courteous Service* paint scheme. Shown in Columbus, Ohio in January of 1973. *(Paul C. Winters)*

SAL XML 28127, series 28000-28499
▲ With the 28000 series ventilated boxcars off the roster, the SAL used the vacant number series for these new boxcars, purchased in 1966 from American Car and Foundry. These cars were delivered without roofwalks and with low mounted brake wheels. They were 50'6" long and were equipped with 10' Youngstown plug doors. Cars 28000-28199 had 20" Freightmaster cushioning device. Note the trademark ACF "stiffeners" to the right of the door. Shown at Wildwood, Fla. in April of 1973. *(George Eicheberger)*

SAL XML 28203, series 28000-28499
▼ Cars 28200-28499 were delivered with 20" Keystone cushioned underframes. This particular shot clearly shows the American Car and Foundry diagonally paneled roof. Given their relative newness at the time of the merger, these cars survived a long time in their original paint scheme, such that when railfans think of "Green Hornets," these cars come to mind. Paper products, glass products, chemicals, food products, cosmetics and tobacco were but a few of the products shipped in these cars. Shown on the LV in November of 1968. *(Bill Folsom collection)*

SAL XML 28500, series 28500-28799

▲ Apparently the Seaboard was impressed with this car design enough that it went to long time builder Pullman-Standard for another 150 cars, delivered in late 1966. Note that this series, along with the previous series, were the only boxcars delivered without roofwalks and with the low mounted brake wheels. These cars had 20" Keystone cushioned underframes. Shown here, brand new, outside the Bessemer, Ala. Pullman-Standard plant in November of 1966. *(Jim Gibson)*

SAL XML 28537, series 28500-28799

▲ Here is a shot of one of these cars after a few years of service. Even dirty, the "Green Hornet" paint scheme looked smart. The car's good equipment made it very popular with shippers. As a result, like many of its brethren, this car is in assigned service. While some railroads painted plug doors to contrast with the car, the SAL painted them the same color as the car. Shown in Uceta Yard in Tampa, Fla. on June 2, 1974. *(George Eichelberger)*

SAL XML 28780, series 28500-28799

▼ A very nice broad side shot of the same cars series, again new at the Pullman-Standard plant in Bessemer, Ala. New, this car is a very eye catching car with its green paint and yellow lettering. While these cars appear to be identical to the previous series, differences in roof and end types, as well as the lack of the side stiffener right of the door, mark them as being built by a different builder. These were the last new boxcars delivered to the SAL. Shown in December of 1966. *(Jim Gibson)*

SAL XM 10090, series 10000-10199, class AF

▲ Not a common car type on the SAL, this car was the first 50 foot, double door car owned by the railroad. Built in 1938 by Pullman-Standard, these cars had a door opening of 12'6", an inside height of 10'1", and a capacity of 50 tons. They were unusual, in that they had flat ends, rather than the Dreadnaught ends common in this period. Shown at Columbus, Ohio in April of 1962.

(*Paul C. Winters*)

SAL XML 15519, series 15500-15599

▼ This 50 foot, 70 ton double plug door box was built by American Car and Foundry in 1964. These cars were 70 ton capacity, had 30" ACF Freightmaster cushioning and Evans DF-2 lading anchoring. This car, and the next car, illustrate the second, 1963 version of the "Green Hornet" paint scheme. Their 16' wide door openings made them ideal for certain types of paper product service. Note the extended roofwalk over the ends. Shown here at Apex, N. C., in December of 1974. (*Warren Calloway*)

62

SAL XML 16478, series 16300-16549

▲ In 1964, the SAL went to American Car and Foundry for 250 of these 50' cars with a pair of 8' plug doors. Half of these cars, 16300-16424, had 20" Keystone cushioned underframes, while the remainder, 16425-16549, had 20" Hydra-cushion underframes. All cars had Evans DF-2 load protection belt rails, and had a pine lining 4'6" high. These cars were assigned to paper loading, bagged materials, and packaged oil products. Shown nearly new in August of 1964 in Atlanta, Ga.
(Howard Robins)

BOXCARS
60' BOXCARS

SAL XML 60003, series 60000-60024

▼ Built by Thrall in 1965, these cars were the largest boxcars on the SAL. Having a capacity of 90 tons and a height of 15'3", these cars featured 20" Keystone cushioning devices and beefy 36" wheels. The door opening was 16', where a pair of 8' Youngstown plug doors was fitted. While cars of this type were generally used for auto parts, the SAL used them to handle large rolls of kraft paper. This particular car was assigned to Bowater Paper in Calhoun, Tenn. It is shown here, nearly new, at Tower 55 in Fort Worth, Tex. in August of 1965. *(K. B. King, Richard Yaremko collection)*

ROOF HATCH BOXCARS

SAL LC 13097, series 13000-13099

▲ What looks like a boxcar is, in fact, a specialty car. Classified "LC" by the AAR, this car is a roof hatch boxcar designed to carry powdered material as bulk phosphate, clay and kaolin. Initially built in 1944 by Pullman-Standard, these cars were rebuilt from 19500-19699 series of cars in 1965 by the Portsmouth shops. They were 41'10" long inside, had 6' doors, and two round 30" hatches located diagonally on the roof. Shown at Rome, Ga. in February, 1967. *(Bill Folsom)*

SAL LC 13207, series 13100-13334

◄ These roof hatch boxcars were built new by Evans in 1966-67, and featured nailable steel floors. The first 200 cars have a pair of 30" roof hatches, diagonally opposite each other near the ends, while the last 35 cars had four hatches at the ends of the car. As can been seen, phosphate and clay service gets the car very dirty. Shown in Atlanta, Ga. in February of 1965. *(Howard Robins)*

SAL LC 13240, series 13100-13334

▼ Roof hatch boxcars were the result of an idea of using a house car to ship bulk material one way while returning with general freight on the backhaul. However, the concept was flawed, as the bulk material hauled, like phosphate, left the interior of these cars very dirty, the boxcar design made unloading difficult, and the nailable steel floors allowed some powdered cargo to leak. Caulking the floor seams solved the last problem. Shown at Russell, Ky. in June of 1970 moving "interior" phosphate bound to the Midwest, rather than for export. *(George Eichelberger)*

SAL RBLD 593491, series 593415-593459

▲ This car, really an insulated boxcar, was leased from Fruit Growers Express. With its load protection devices, load dividers, roller bearing trucks and cushioned underframe, it is the high water mark of SAL refrigerator cars. Used to transport a large variety of perishable and temperature sensitive items, this particular car is assigned to perishable service out of Wildwood, Fla. One can only speculate on the cargo as it passes through this northern locality in a spring snow in April of 1966. *(Rail Data Services)*

65

SAL SM 3050, series 3020-3054, class S1

▼ While one generally does not think of the SAL as owning stock cars, they did have them. However, as the live stock traffic dwindled on the East Coast, the SAL scrapped or rebuilt their fleets. This car is one of only 13 in revenue service when the photo was taken. This car was built by Pullman in 1926 and is listed as having an 80 ton capacity. Taken in New Brunswick, N.J., in March of 1965.

(Dr. Art Peterson)

**SAL VM 28352,
series 28000-29249, class V9**

▶ This is an old shot of an old car that one would expect the Seaboard to have. Built in 1922, and known to modelers as "watermelon cars," these cars were used for a variety of fruit and produce service where refrigeration was not an issue. This car was 36'9" long, and had a capacity of 40 tons. At one time, the Seaboard had over 10,000 ventilated boxcars. By 1966, only two ventilated boxcars were still in revenue service. Shown at Lawrence, Kan. in November of 1955. (*Don Ball collection*)

VENTILATOR CARS

SAL VM 79977, series 79000-79999, class V-10

▼ This is another class of ventilated boxcars. Notice the ventilators in the ends of the car. The sides are plywood, but were originally wood sheathed. This particular car was built in 1923, and had the capacity of 40 tons. It was 37' long. Improved roads resulted in the loss of produce traffic to trucks, such that the remaining traffic was either handled in ice reefers used in ventilator service (with the ice hatches propped open) or TOFC trailers. Shown at Bradenton, Fla. on an unknown date.

(*Emery Gulash, Joseph Oates collection*)

SAL LO 7084, series 7050-7099

▲ Among the more unusual covered hoppers that were owned by the SAL were these 100-ton cars purchased in 1965 from General American Transportation. These cars were only 34'1" long., and were essentially a tank car used as a hopper. Designed to handle dry, powdered materials, these cars worked on the principle that powder flows like a fluid when moved by compressed air. The tank diameter was 10'8", and there was only one compartment. Shown at Wildwood, Fla. on June 3, 1973.

(Stan Jackowski)

SAL LO 7097, series 7050-7099

▼ As one might surmise from the appearance of these cars, they carried caustic material. The assignment manual shows the entire series assigned to Lehigh Cement, in Lehigh, Florida. Some of these cars are still in use today by owner CSX in sludge service. The CB&Q had similar cars, numbered 84950-84999. Shown in Wildwood, Fla. in March of 1970.

(Howard Robins)

SAL LO 7101, series 7100-7109

▲ The SAL purchased its first Airslide hoppers in 1960 from General American. They were one bay cars, with inside length of 29'6" and a capacity of 77 tons. These cars were assigned to handle clean lading, as malt, flour, and sugar. This particular car was assigned to flour loading at Peavey Mills, in Alton, Ill. Shown in Hollis, Ill. on May 10, 1980. *(George Eichelberger)*

SAL LO 7118, series 7110-7129

▼ In 1962, the SAL returned to General American for 20 more one compartment Airslide hoppers identical to the previous series. Compressed air was used to create a fluid bed in conjunction with a special fabric bed to allow powdered materials to easily slide in unloading, hence the name "Airslide." The net effect was reduced lading "clingage" and contamination. This car was assigned to flour service. Shown in Tampa, Fla. on March 17, 1973. *(Stan Jackowski)*

SAL LO 7141, series 7125-7144

▲ The SAL saw the advantages of Airslide hoppers, for they went back to General American in 1964 to purchase the larger two bay cars. These cars had an inside length of 48'11" and a capacity of 90 tons. Like all the Seaboard's other Airslides, these cars spent their lives in assigned service. This particular car was assigned to American Sugar in Three Oaks, La. Shown at Wildwood, Fla. at a scrap company in April of 1987. *(Joseph Oates)*

SAL LO 7823, series 7600-7999

▼ The SAL had a large fleet of 29'3" two bay, two compartment, 70 ton covered hoppers. These cars had eight 36"x36" square hatches. These cars were built in 1953 by Pullman-Standard at their Butler, Pa. plant. Cars of this type were very important to the SAL, as a large percentage of its business was phosphate, fertilizer, clay, cement, fishmeal, chemicals and other commodities that used standard covered hoppers. This particular car was assigned to fishmeal loading out of Savannah, Ga. Shown at Hamlet, N. C. in August 1976. *(Warren Calloway)*

SAL LO 8838, series 8650-8849

▲ These cars were purchased from American Car and Foundry in 1956. They were also 29'3" two bay, two compartment, 70 ton covered hoppers, with eight 36"x36" square hatches. This particular car was assigned to silica loading out of Plant City, Fla. This car illustrates the standard covered hopper paint scheme for all two bay cars, which featured a gray body with black reporting marks and black 9" road name on the upper portion of the sides. Shown in Valrico, Fla. on June 9, 1973. *(Stan Jackowski)*

SAL LO 30333, series 30000-30549

▼ In 1957, the SAL ordered 500 of these cars from American Car and Foundry for itself, and another 50 of these cars for the Macon, Dublin and Savannah. These cars were 35'9" long and rated for 70 tons and 2006 cu. ft. They had eight square 36x36" hatches, four hoppers and two compartments. Assigned to cement, silica and clay loading, most of these cars got dirty to the point where the railroad name is barely visible, as shown here. Shown at an unknown location in October of 1975.

(Warren Calloway)

SAL LO 30690, series 30550-30749

▲ In 1960, the SAL returned to Pullman-Standard for 250 new covered hoppers of the PS-2 design to cover its growing cement and clay business. These cars were 35' 11" long and featured eight 30" diameter round hatch-es, 4 hoppers and two compartments. Delivered with roller bearing trucks, these cars were rated at 70 tons and 2007 cu. ft. Shown in Tampa, Fla. in December of 1978. *(George Eichelberger)*

SAL LO 30776, series 30750-30949

▲ The first fifty foot PS-2 covered hoppers owned by the SAL were these 200 cars, purchased from Pullman-Standard in 1964. Capacity is listed at 100 tons and 2929 cu. ft. These cars featured ten round roof hatches 30" in diameter, six hoppers, three compartments and roller bearing trucks. Like their shorter predecessors, these cars saw a variety of service, especially in cement, clay, silica, phosphate and feed loading. Shown in Tampa, Fla., on April 6, 1987. *(George Eichelberger)*

SAL LO 31069, series 30950-31099

▼ Pullman-Standard delivered another 150 PS-2 covered hoppers to the Seaboard in 1964. The features of these cars are virtually identical to the previous series, with the exception of the roof hatches, which have an equal spacing. Shown in Atlanta, Ga. on November 10, 1984. *(George Eichelberger)*

SAL LO 31316, series 31100-31699

▲ Built by Pullman-Standard in 1966, these cars have three compartments, six hoppers, and have ten circular hatches of 30" diameter. The capacity of these cars is listed as 90 tons and 3,933 cu. ft. The lettering scheme shown is the last covered hopper scheme, with the 24" black billboard road name on the upper sides. The dirty exterior of this car is explained by the fact that it is assigned to Dry Branch, Ga. for clay service. Shown in Asheville, N. C. on December 22, 1984. *(Paul Faulk)*

SAL LO 31583, series 31100-31699

▼ This particular car is a bit cleaner, and is shown here, in Raleigh, N. C., near the end of the SCL's existence, some 16 years after being delivered to the Seaboard. The cleaner exterior of this car can be explained by the fact that it was assigned for feed loading to Ralston-Purina in Richmond, Va. These cars are basically an extended height version of the previous series, standing at 14' 7" above the rails, versus 12'6" of the standard height PS-2 covered hopper. Shown in May of 1982. *(Warren Calloway)*

SAL LO 31952, series 31700-31999

▲ The high PS-2 cars must have been successful in their intended service, for in 1967, the SAL went back to Pullman-Standard for another 200 cars, which came from their Butler, Pa. plant. These cars were virtually identi- cal to the previous series. This particular car is assigned to general service and is shown at East Tampa, Fla. in June of 1973. *(George Eichelberger)*

SAL LO 32389, series 32000-32499

▲ Built in 1967, there were 500 of these cars delivered to the SAL from Pullman-Standard's Bessemer Ala. plant. Rated at 100 tons and 2929 cu. ft., these cars had three compartments, six hoppers, and ten 30" round hatches, like the previous orders. Most of these cars were in general service, which might include silica, phosphates, clay, chemicals or any variety of dry, pow- dered materials. This car is shown at Hamlet, N. C. on February 27, 1988, in surprisingly good paint, despite its over 21 years of service. *(Paul Faulk)*

SAL LO 32499, series 32000-32499

▼ You may very well be looking at the very last freight car ever delivered to the Seaboard Air Line. Obviously the last car of this series, this car is shown new, just outside the Pullman-Standard plant in Bessemer, Ala., just prior to delivery. This final order brought the total number of these type cars to 750 on the Seaboard. The date on the slide is February of 1967. This is an excellent shot of what these cars looked like when new. *(Jim Gibson)*

SAL LO 35059, series 35025-35124

▲ Besides phosphates, clay and chemicals, the Seaboard had a fairly substantial business in grain. To handle this traffic, the SAL invested in a group of high cubic capacity aluminum covered hoppers. These cars, delivered from Magor in 1964, were 54'2" long, and were rated at 100 tons and 4725 cu. ft. These cars were equipped with three compartments, six hoppers, and twelve 30" diameter roof hatches. This particular car is shown in Uceta yard, in Tampa, Fla. in February of 1975. *(George Eichelberger)*

SAL LO 35178, series 35125-35224

▼ With the success of the first cars of this type, the Seaboard went back to Magor in 1966 for another 100 covered hoppers. Also built out of aluminum, they were virtually identical to the previous series. The aluminum sides tended to darken with age and service, such that it is very difficult to see the lettering on many of these cars. This clean car is shown in Tampa, Fla., on July 4, 1973. *(Stan Jackowski)*

SAL LO 35703, series 35700-35704

▼ These particular cars were the only examples of American Car and Foundry "round type, center flow" covered hoppers on the SAL roster. Built in 1965, these cars were 100 ton, three hopper, three compartment cars of 3,500 cu. ft. capacity with six 30" diameter roof hatches. Originally, the SAL had ordered the six hopper version of this car, which were delivered in 1962 as series 35800-35804. The SAL was unhappy with the original cars and all were returned to ACF and replaced by these cars. Shown at Wildwood, Fla. in June of 1973. *(George Eichelberger)*

SAL LO 35806, series 35805-35899
▲ Purchased in 1962 from Magor Car, these cars had a capacity of 90 tons and 3818 cu. ft. These cars were 47'8" long and 14' 7" tall, and were used for general service. Shown at Rebecca, Ga. on December 29, 1967. *(Larry Goolsby)*

SAL LO 35861, series 35805-35899
▼ Another shot of the 90 ton Magor covered hoppers. Most of these cars survived in their SAL delivery paint for quite some time, and most got very dirty. This shot, and the previous shot, are good examples of that paint scheme, which was quite attractive. Shown on the PRR at Columbus, Ohio, in October of 1962. *(Paul C. Winters)*

SAL LO 35944, series 35900-35999
▼ The SAL had its share of lower density shipments, and found that it was in need of some higher cubic capacity covered hoppers. These cars, purchased new from Magor in 1960, were built of Cor-ten steel, and had three compartments and six hoppers, and the predecessors of the previous series. Shown at Uceta Yard in Tampa, Fla. in January of 1975.

(George Eichelberger)

SAL LO 59026, series 58675-59274

▲ The Seaboard had a huge business in phosphate, an ingredient in fertilizer. Processed phosphate rock is a dense, corrosive material sensitive to water. Therefore, it was carried in covered hoppers dedicated to that purpose. These cars had one compartment and four hopper type discharge chutes. The roof had eight roof hatches. These cars were 37' long and stood only 10'9" tall. They were rated at 70 tons and 1912 cu. ft. These particular cars were built by Pullman-Standard in 1951. Shown in Tampa, Fla. on June 9, 1973. *(Stan Jackowski)*

SAL LO 59386, series 59275-59474

▼ Virtually identical to the previous series, the SAL purchased these cars from Pullman-Standard in 1956. This car is very typical of the general appearance of phosphate cars used for "dry rock," as the processed phosphate is called. These cars generally carried processed phosphate from the plants to the shipping docks at Tampa. Sometimes, entire trains of these cars ventured north, carrying phosphate elsewhere. Shown in Tampa, Fla. in December of 1978. *(George Eichelberger)*

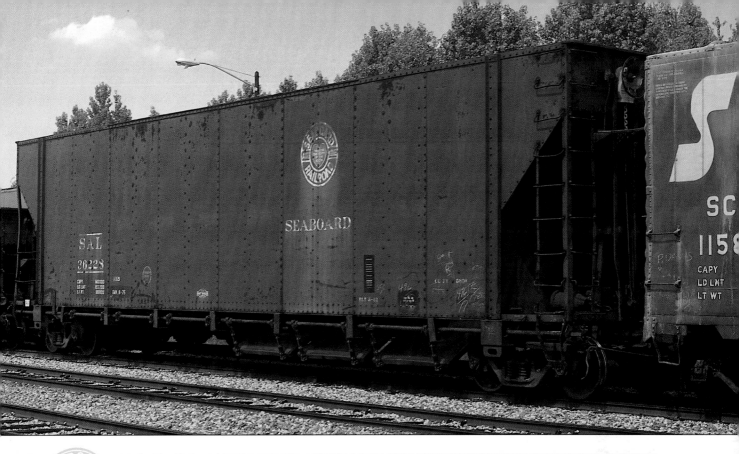

SAL HKS 36228, series 36200-36399

▲ One of the commodities that the SAL hauled in bulk was wood chips. Once considered refuse by saw mills, the demand for this material increased dramatically when processes allowed it to be used for making paper and particle board. Wood chips could be hauled nicely in open hoppers, but their light weight resulted in poor utilization of the tonnage capacity of the cars. The answer is in the development of high cubic capacity cars like these. Shown in Greenville, S. C. on September 24, 1976. *(Paul Faulk)*

SAL HKS 36292, series 36200-36399

▼ This car was part of a 200 car order delivered to the SAL in 1962 from Greenville Car. These cars had a cubic capacity of 5,850 cu. ft. and 75 tons. They were 56' 10" long and had 12 drop doors in the bottom. Cars that were very similar to this design were common in the Southeast, but the drop doors were unique to the SAL. Usually captive to on line service, this particular car is shown far from home at Belt Line Jct. in Reading, Pa. on May 22, 1977. *(Craig Bossler)*

SAL HKS 36404, series 36400-36499

▲ In 1966, the Seaboard returned to Greenville Car for more cars of the same design as the previous series. These cars were identical in nearly all respects except for the low mounted brake wheel and improved side panel stiffeners. While light, wood chips could be quite heavy when wet, and as a result, could play havoc with the weight distribution in the car. This car features the 24" billboard lettering, as opposed to the previous series. Shown in Charleston, S. C. on February 26, 1977.

(Joe Kmetz, coll. of Bill Folsom)

SAL HT 37030, series 37000-37199

▼ In 1966, the Portsmouth, Va. shops of the SAL began a program to upgrade some of its older hoppers. Some members of the offset sided series 37600-38199 built in 1948 were upgraded with rib sides to create this new series of 200 cars. These cars were 41'3" long, rated at 77 tons, and could carry 2860 cu. ft. Shown in October of 1976 at Apex, N. C.

(Warren Calloway)

78

SAL HT 38944, series 38650-39149

▲ These cars, built in 1957 by Pullman-Standard at Butler, Pa., were 40'8" long, could hold 2773 cu. ft and could carry 70 tons. In spite of the fact that many of these cars were candidates for rebuilding programs, a large number survived into the mid 1970's. This car is shown with the delivery paint scheme at Apex, N. C. in October of 1976.

(Warren Calloway)

SAL HT 38982, series 38650-39149

▼ From the same series, this car shows a modified paint scheme. While the Seaboard is not thought of as a coal carrier, it had a number of hoppers for hauling sand and gravel from the many on line pits. In addition to sand and gravel, these cars hauled crushed stone and ballast. The coal the SAL did haul came from connections such as the C&O, N&W and Clinchfield. This car is shown basking in the warm Florida sun at Live Oak in March of 1970. *(Howard Robins)*

SAL HT 39119, series 38650-39149

▲ Here is a great shot of the "typical" Seaboard open top triple hopper car as so many modelers and railfans know it. One of a series of 500 cars, this car is a good representative of the 2650 cars built to the AAR design by various builders between 1948 and 1958. Shown in Atlanta, Ga. in March of 1969. *(Howard Robins)*

SAL HT 39165, series 39150-39849

▼ Virtually identical to the previous series, this car is from a group of 700 cars built by Pullman in 1958 at their Butler, Pa. plant. The car still retains its original paint, albeit modified with re-weigh stencils and weathering, in this shot taken at Greenville, S. C. in the ex-P&N yard on September 24, 1976. *(Paul Faulk)*

SAL HT 39366, series 39150-39849

▼ This car was part of a group of 700 cars built by Pullman-Standard at Butler, Pa. in 1958. These cars were rated at 70 tons and 2,773 cu. ft. loaded level. The paint scheme, with the large, stenciled lettering, is not the deliv-ery scheme. This car was assigned for loading out of Live Oak, Fla. The markings above the middle bay, however, indicate the car is to be sold for scrap. Shown on April 5, 1980 at Hamlet, N. C. *(Bob Graham)*

SAL HT 39493, series 39150-39849

▲ Here is a nice photo of one of the offset triple hoppers from above. This shot does a great job of showing the interior of the car. Note the re-enforcing ribs from the inside. Note also, the evidence of "load wear," which indicates the car has been carrying dense materials that were not loaded completely to the top of the car. Shown in Enola, Pa. on September 5, 1971. *(Craig Bossler)*

SAL HT 40032, series 40000-40499

▼ Built by American Car and Foundry in 1960, these cars were the first triple rib sided hopper cars delivered to the Seaboard. These cars were rated at 70 tons and 2700 cu. ft, and came equipped with roller bearing trucks. Though barely visible in the photograph, these cars had re-enforced side panels. This paint scheme, featuring the large road name, is not the delivery paint scheme. Shown in December of 1983. *(Bill Folsom)*

SAL HT 40416, series 40000-40499

▲ These rib sided hoppers proved to be very successful, so much so that they provided the template and genesis for the Seaboard's hopper car rebuilding program of 1966. Many lasted, unaltered, well into the early 1980's. Like their offset sided brethren, these cars served their owner well hauling sand, gravel, crushed stone, ballast and coal. This car sports the delivery paint scheme as shown in October of 1975 in Apex, N. C. *(Warren Calloway)*

SAL HM 56814, series 56800-56899

▼ These cars, modified from the 37100-37399 series hoppers in 1959 by the Portsmouth shops, were 38'5" long outside, but only 29'10" long inside. They were rated at 70 tons and 1544 cu. ft. Known as "wet rock" cars, they have the same exterior length (40') as triple hoppers, but the same interior length (29') as twin hoppers, with steep slope sheets going nearly to the top. The space at either end is taken up with a large platform and screening, which allows spilled material to fall to the ground and not overload the car. Shown in Tampa, Fla. on January 4, 1974. *(George Eichelberger)*

SAL HM 56921, series 56900-57199

▲ This particular series of cars was purchased new from Bethlehem Steel in 1957. These cars are nearly identical to the previous series. The gray paint scheme was very serviceable, since phosphate quickly stained these cars with white streaks. Notice the stenciling is different from the previous shot. Shown in Tampa, Fla. on November 16, 1974. *(George Eichelberger)*

SAL HM 57368, series 57200-57374

▼ In 1962, the SAL went to Greenville Car for 175 of these cars. They differ from the previous designs by being slightly longer and taller. However, they are still rated at 70 tons and only slightly more cu. ft. (1550). Notice the car is loaded. "Wet rock" cars were used to handle raw phosphate, really a muddy slurry, from the mines to the washer, or washed phosphate, known as "wet rock" to plants for further processing. Shown at Mulberry, Fla. in July of 1977. *(George Eichelberger)*

SAL HM 57423, series 57375-57499

▼ This car represents another order of 125 cars, also built by Greenville in 1962. These cars are identical to the previous series, except for the roller bearing trucks. While "wet rock" cars tended to stay in dedicated service in the "Bone Valley " mining district of central Florida most of their careers, this car is shown in sand service in nearby Venice Fla., in May of 1973.

(George Eichelberger)

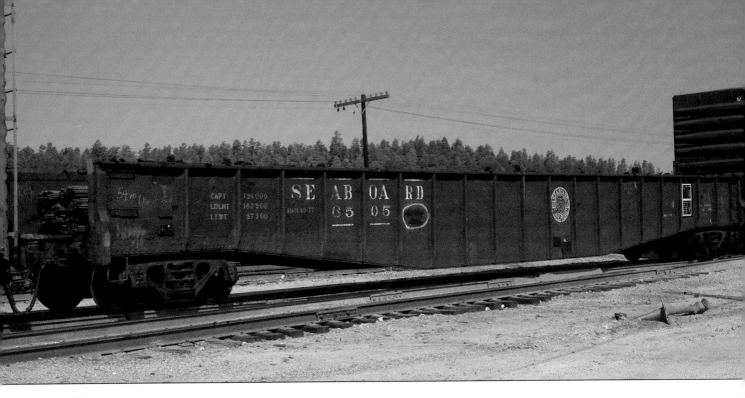

GONDOLAS

SAL GB 6505, series 6500-6549

84 ▲ These cars were 65' mill gondolas, 70-ton capacity, with an inside height of 3'6". They were built by Pullman-Standard in 1949 to the AAR design. Certainly, these cars earned their keep hauling steel shapes out of Birmingham, Ala. Here, we see one of them at Lakeland, Fla. on July 5, 1981; moving a load of steel re-bar. *(R. Stone, Joseph Oates collection)*

SAL GB 6528, series 6500-6549

▼ Besides steel structural shapes, mill gondolas were used in a variety of services, such as hauling pipe and poles. Their drop ends made them especially valuable for hauling long cargo, with the use of idler flats. Location unknown, December 1981. *(Matt Herson)*

SAL GB 6677, series 6550-6749

▲ In addition to the usual steel shapes, the SAL also handled coiled steel out of Birmingham. Not a huge source of traffic, the SAL chose to handle this traffic by modifying nine cars from this series with roof covers. This particular car was assigned to TCI in Birmingham, Ala. Shown in Tampa, Fla. in March of 1970. *(Stan Jackowski)*

SAL GB 6695, series 6550-6749

▼ This car was one of a series of 200 cars, built by Magor in 1957. It was 41'6" long inside with an inside height of 4'6" and a capacity of 70 tons. Like most gondolas, these cars saw rough service, as evidenced by the "swaybacked" appearance of this car. The gray paint scheme indicates that this particular car was designated for mud service, really a limerock slurry, to Florida Portland Cement in Tampa, Fla., where it was photographed in October of 1973. *(George Eichelberger)*

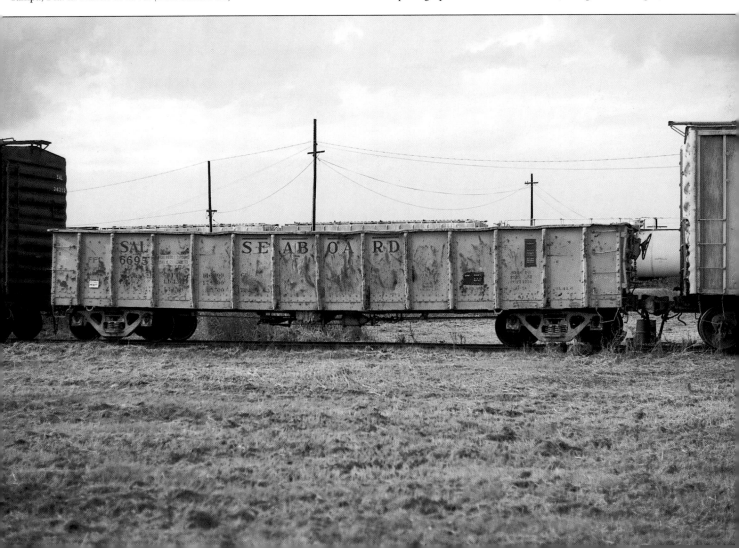

SAL GB 6758, series 6750-6949

▲ This car was a member of a series of 200 cars, built by Magor in 1958. Apparently, the SAL was satisfied with the previous order, as this group of cars was identical to the previous series. Some of these cars, like the previous series, were modified with a removable steel roof, others were designated for "mud" service, while others were modified for "stump" service. This is a stump car, as evidenced by the load and the slots in the sides at the floor level. Photographed in Lakeland, Fla., on August 3, 1991. *(Stan Jackowski)*

SAL GB 6857, series 6750-6949

▼ Pine stumps had economic value for the high rosin content, which was extracted to make turpentine and nitrocellulose. While not necessarily lucrative, it was a source of stable traffic. Nearly every town in the "pine belt" had a couple of these cars in a siding for a contractor who was digging stumps from a previously logged area. A stump assignment meant rough service that generally rendered the car unfit for anything else. Shown at Hamlet, N. C. on January 2, 1984. *(Larry Goolsby)*

SAL GB 6865, series 6750-6949

▲ Stump wood was an important commodity until increasing expenses in the mid to late 1980's made the process too costly, and this stable traffic source vanished from the rails. The car is shown at Hamlet, N. C. on September 29, 1985. Several of these cars were assigned to that location for stump loading around that area. *(Bob Graham)*

SAL GBR 6938, series 6750-6949

▼ The SAL had several can manufacturers on line, and as a result, moved a fair amount of coiled tinplate. This necessitated covered gondolas to handle the material. Again, the SAL elected to modify existing cars with covers. Shown in Tampa, Fla. on January 20, 1974.
(Stan Jackowski, George Eichelberger collection)

SAL GBSR 6954, series 6950-6959

▼ This covered gondola was purchased new from Thrall in 1962. It was 52'1 1/4" inside, with an inside height of 4' 6" and a capacity of 70 tons. These cars had four movable interior bulkheads and a 10" Freightmaster hydraulic cushioned underframe. As expected, these cars handled rolled tinplate, but also rolled steel for TCI out of Birmingham, Ala. Shown in Tampa, Fla. on November 4, 1973.
(Stan Jackowski, George Eichelberger collection)

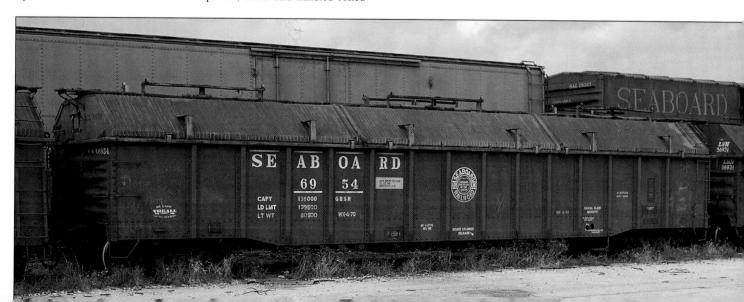

SAL GB 90124, series 90100-90299

▲ These gondolas were built in 1951 as a 200 car order from Bethlehem Steel. Rated 50 tons and 1150 cu ft, these cars were known as "low sided" gondolas, having an interior height of only 2'11". They were 41'6" long inside and rated at 70 tons. Gondolas generally served yeoman service, and hauled all types of freight. Some members of this class were equipped with containers. Shown in Florence, S. C. on June 20, 1981. *(Paul Faulk)*

SAL GB 90448, series 90300-90599

▲ Another group of "low sided" gondolas, virtually identical to the previous series, except they were built in 1952 by Pullman-Standard at their Butler, Pa. plant. This car illustrates the standard SAL gondola paint scheme. Sand typically moved in gondolas in the Southeast. Unloading these solid bottom cars was not easy, for even if clamshell or some other machine did it, some muscle power was still necessary to completely empty the car. Shown in Yeoman Yard at Tampa, Fla. in May of 1975. *(George Eichelberger)*

SAL GB 90989, series 90600-90999

▼ This series of 300 "low sided" gondolas was rebuilt by the Portsmouth, Va. shops in 1952 from 96000, 97000, 98000 and 99000 series gondolas. Again, the dimensions and ratings are the same as the previous series. This particular car shows the remains of the "stencil" paint scheme, evidence of the hard service a gondola typically sees. It is still in maintenance of way service for CSX at Laurens, S. C. on January 27, 1990. *(Paul Faulk)*

SAL GB 91708, series 91400-91899

▲ In addition to "low sided" gondolas, the SAL also had "high sided" gondolas. These cars were built by Bethlehem Steel in 1951 and were 4'6" tall inside, giving another 19" of siding capacity. Rated at 55 tons and 1772 cu ft, these cars were also 41'6" long inside. This is a nice side view far from home in Reading, Pa. on April 12, 1978. *(Craig Bossler)*

SAL GB 91741, series 91400-91899

▼ Another nice view of a "high sided" gondola. Like their "low sided" brethren, these cars saw all kinds of service. High sided cars were generally suited for bulkier, less dense materials. All totaled, the SAL had 1510 high sided cars and 3110 low sided cars. Shown in February of 1975. *(George Eichelberger)*

SAL GB 92030, series 91900-92199

▼ This car is a part of a lot of 300 "high side" gondolas built by Pullman-Standard at Butler, Pa. in 1952. Having only slight differences from the previous series built by Bethlehem Steel, these cars are built to an SAL specification for gondolas established in 1950. Evidence of the heavy use and abuse that gondolas take can be easily seen on the sides of this car. Shown in Reading, Pa. on September 2, 1973. *(Craig Bossler)*

SAL GB 93620, series 93400-94699

▲ This is a large group of "low sided" gondolas rebuilt by the Portsmouth shops from older gondolas in 1954. The rock load shows the advantage of the low sides quite well, in that sides were needed to keep the load in the car, while the low sides made loading and unloading easier. This shot shows the solid floors and ends. Shown in Camden, S. C. on October 6, 1978, as it heads north in the consist of SCL train 594. *(Paul Faulk)*

SAL GB 93895, series 93700-94999

▼ Here is another "low sided" gondola, this one being from a group rebuilt in 1955. The series of cars that were used for the rebuilds date back to 1926. The sand load would now be shipped in hoppers to avoid the time consuming, labor intensive task of unloading of a solid bottom gondola. Shown in May of 1965 at an unknown location. *(Dr. Art Peterson)*

SAL GB 95332, series 95000-95699, class G9

▼ Our final series of "low sided" gondolas was built in 1957 by Bethlehem Steel to the standard design. This group of 700 cars was identical to all the other "low sided" cars, except for lading straps above each side rib. This particular car is shown in Mulberry, Fla. in September of 1985, and lacks the usual herald, having the name and number repeated instead.

(G. H. Anderson, George Eichelberger collection)

SAL FM 4712, series 4700-4724

▲ These cars were built by Thrall in 1960 and were 49'7" in length, with a bulkhead height of 18", and a capacity of 90 tons. Here we see 4712 hauling the remains of SAL F-3 4027 back into Hamlet, N. C. on July 27, 1966. The 4027 was destroyed in a head-on collision at Cherryville, N. C. on July 17 when a train ran a meet order. *(Wiley Bryan, Warren Calloway collection)*

SAL FM 4717, series 4700-4724

▼ Here is another photo of the low bulkhead flat cars. These cars were originally purchased to move coiled tinplate. When found to be unsuitable for that service, they were assigned to slab granite service out of Elberton, Georgia. Shown in Atlanta, Ga. on April 1, 1977, on an inbound SCL train at Howells yard.

(George Eichelberger)

SAL FM 47193, series 47100-47199, class F6

▲ This is one of 200 flatcars purchased from Greenville in 1942. Like most of the SAL's open flat cars, they were 50' long and rated at 50 tons. They were 3'8" above the rails. Most general service flats saw all kinds of service, and were frequent candidates for use in maintenance of way service. This car is shown here moving a piece of track equipment in Raleigh, N. C. on March 23, 1983. *(George Eichelberger)*

SAL FMS 47345, series 47200-47499, class F6

▼ Originally built in 1945 by Bethlehem Steel as part of a series of ordinary flat cars, this car had bulkheads added by the Portsmouth shops in 1953. Interior height was 6', with 44'10" of clearance between the bulkheads. These cars were rated at 50 tons, and were assigned to Reynolds Metal in Richmond, Va. What appear to be diagonal braces on the left end of the car are actually loose boards as the car waits for the end in the scrap line at Hamlet, N. C. on April 5, 1980. *(Bob Graham)*

92

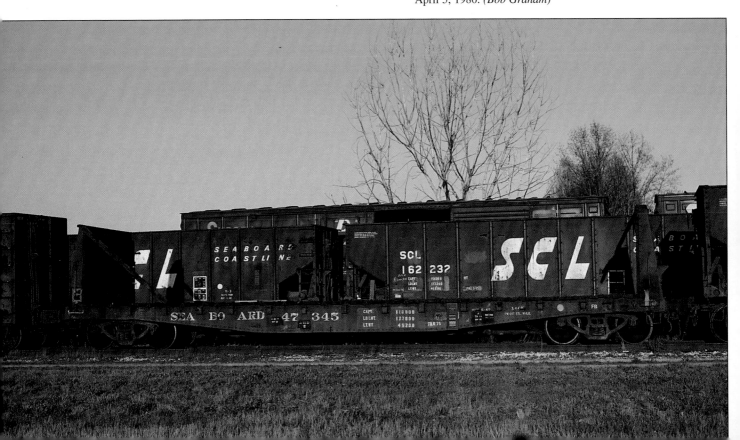

SAL FMS 47387, series 47200-47499, class F6

▲ These cars were part of a large order of 300 flat cars built in 1945 by Bethlehem Steel. They were rated at 50 tons, were 50'9" long and stood 3'8" above the rails. This car also appears to have drafted into maintenance of way service. Shown in Perry, Fla. on May 24, 1974.

(Stan Jackowski, George Eichelberger collection)

SAL FMS 48109, series 48100-48124

▼ In 1962, the SAL went to Ortner for these bulkhead flatcars. They had 48'6" of clear space between the bulkheads, stood 11'9" tall, and were rated at 70 tons. They had Waugh cushioned underframes, steel floors, roller bearing trucks and chain boxes on the left side of the car. Note the green paint scheme with yellow lettering, like the cushioned underframe boxcars. Shown in Tampa, Fla. at Uceta Yard on December 30, 1973. *(Stan Jackowski, coll. of George Eichelberger)*

93

SAL FMS 48119, series 48100-48124

▲ Another nice shot of one of the Ortner flat cars. Although there were only 25 of these cars, their cushioned underframes and green paint schemes made them attractive, eye catching cars. This particular car shows the bulkhead design and chain boxes along the sides very well. This car was one of a group of 20 cars assigned for loading wallboard at Kaiser Gypsum at North Shore, Fla. Shown on April 5, 1980 at Hamlet, N. C.

(Bob Graham)

SAL FMS 48163, series 48125-48274

▼ Here is an example of one of 150 bulkhead flat cars built in 1964 by Thrall. These cars had 61' of clearance between the bulkheads and stood 14'10" above the rails. The cars had a capacity of 90 tons, and rode on roller bearing trucks with beefy 38" wheels. There were 14 chains and winches for load securement on each side of the car, which can be seen over the sides of the load. Shown in Allentown, Pa. on March 15, 1987.

(Olev Taremae)

94

SAL FMS 48321, series 48275-48324

▲ Bulkhead lumber cars were the answer to the problem of moving lumber by rail. If secured to a regular flat car, the load is subject to shifting at the ends. If loaded in double door boxcars, there was the difficulty of loading and unloading. This car was part of a group of 50 built as a follow-up order in 1967 by Thrall. They are identical to the previous series. Shown at an unknown location earning revenue for its owner in May of 1973. *(George Eichelberger)*

SAL FMS 48733, series 48700-48749

▼ The last flat cars delivered to the SAL were these monsters, built by Thrall in 1967. These 50 cars had 70' of clearance between the bulkheads, and stood 14'10" tall. Equipped with 16 chain pockets per side, these cars had Freightmaster 10" hydraulic cushioning devices and roller bearing trucks with 38" diameter wheels. These cars represented the state of the art in bulkhead flats when delivered. Note the white stripe in the center of the car, which serves as a loading guide. Shown at Rocky Mount, N. C., on July 8, 1979. *(Paul Faulk)*

SAL LP 42901, series 42900-42924

▲ Magor Car built these cars in 1956 for the Macon, Dublin and Savannah. Delivered as their 5000-5024, these cars featured 38' of space between the bulkheads and could carry nearly 22 cords of pulpwood. They stood 11 feet tall. This car is a real survivor, having lasted through three decades and four mergers. Shown at Plant City, Fla. on June 12, 1988. *(George Eichelberger)*

SAL LP 44602, series 44500-44799

▼ The importance of the pulpwood business to the SAL can be seen in the fact that the road continued to purchase new cars right up until the merger. In 1966, the SAL went to Magor Car for 300 50' pulpwood cars of this design. Standing 12'6" tall, these cars could carry nearly 33 cords of wood and were rated at 70 tons. These cars were state of the art design, complete with roller bearing trucks. Shown at Raleigh, N.C. in April of 1984 in the delivery paint scheme. *(Warren Calloway)*

SAL LP 44777, series 44500-44799

▲ This nice down-on photo of one of the Magor pulpwood cars shows the V-shaped floors that make pulpwood cars distinctive from bulkhead flats. The floor is sloped to slant the wood inward to keep it on the car in transit. The white lines on the bulkheads indicate the car centerline. When handled in trains, pulpwood cars were restricted to no more than 50 MPH to avoid shifting and loss of loads. Care was always taken in meeting trains with pulpwood, since the load could fall off into the path of the on-coming train. Shown in Wadesboro, N.C. on August 17, 1977. *(Paul Faulk)*

SAL LP 44880, series 44800-44999

▼ This series, identical to the previous series, was actually built the year before, in 1965. Note the white lines at the top of the bulkheads. These indicate how high the load can go. These cars were fairly narrow by design, at only 9'2" wide, to keep the loads in place. However, yard operators occasionally exceeded the height and width, so it was common to find pieces of pulpwood along the right of way. Shown in Atlanta, Ga. on October 25, 1987.

(Bill Folsom, Jim Kinkaid collection)

SAL LP 45309, series 45300-45599
▲ In 1957, the Seaboard went to Greenville Car for 300 of these cars. These cars measured 50' between bulkheads, were 11'6" high, and could hold 70 tons and nearly 31 cords of wood. Note the car has roller bearing trucks. Pulpwood is the raw material for making paper pulp, and the SAL had many on-line paper mills. Pulpwood cars are called "woodracks" on the SAL. Shown at Raleigh, N. C. in February of 1976. *(Warren Calloway)*

SAL LP 45457, series 45300-45599
▼ Here is a shot of a pulpwood car doing what it was intended to do - hauling pulpwood. The diameter of most of the wood is in the range of 6-12" and the length is 5 feet long. The wood was loaded onto the cars in two parallel rows. Most paper companies had yards scattered about the South where they loaded pulpwood cut in their own forests or purchased wood from independent operators. Here, the wood was unloaded from trucks and re-loaded onto rail cars. Shown in Manchester, Ga. on July 25, 1982. *(Paul Faulk)*

SAL LP 45621, series 45600-45649

▲ Common on other railroads, but not on the SAL, this car is one of only 50 cars ordered from General Steel in 1963. They had an inside length of 45'4", were 12'6" above the rails, and were delivered with roller bearing trucks. Capacity was 70 tons and just over 31 cords of wood. Construction of the car was cast, like the GSC flat cars, of which this car is a version. Note the open ends with no end sheets. Shown at Raleigh, N. C. in February of 1976. *(Warren Calloway)*

SAL LP 45662, series 45650-45899

▼ In 1963, the SAL received 250 of these cars from Thrall. They were rated at 70 tons and could carry nearly 31 cords of wood. They were 50' long inside the bulkheads, and were 9'3" wide and stood 11'6" tall. Delivered on roller bearing trucks, cars of this basic design were the most numerous 50' pulpwood car on the SAL. Conversion of paper pulp mills to "long wood" logs like those on the truck in the background has resulted in a steady decline in "short wood" cars. Shown in Georgianna, Ala. in October of 1988. *(George Eichelberger)*

 ## AUTORACK CARS

SAL FA number unknown, series variable

▲ The SAL was an early user of autoracks, with both bi-level and tri-level cars built by Whitehead and Kales, Paragon and Dana. While grime makes it impossible to determine the number of this rack, Trailer Train installed these racks on whatever cars were handy, resulting in a disjunct numbers. A frequent assignment of these bi-level cars was to the Ford-Norfolk plant, where they were loaded with pick-ups and light trucks. Shown in Columbus, Ohio in February of 1968. *(Paul C. Winters)*

  ## TANK CARS

SAL TM 3003, series 3002-3010

▼ This car is one of only 5 tank cars listed as being in revenue service on the SAL in 1966. By this time, it is doubtful that these cars actually saw revenue service, being used instead in maintenance of way service. The number, W-3003, is not present on any maintenance of way roster, which is probably just an oversight. These cars were originally built in 1920 for the Charlotte Harbor and Northern, a road leased by the SAL in 1925. They carried the same number series, and are listed as 10,000 gallon, 50 ton cars. Taken in Bethune, S.C., April of 1968. *(C. A. Thomas)*

SAL Trailer 30437, series 30402-30901

▲ The Seaboard was an early user of piggyback service, running its first, all-piggyback trains with the PRR. This is a typical SAL piggyback trailer, of the 40' variety built by Great Dane. Note the nose doors, used for ventilation. These insulated trailers ultimately replaced ventilator cars for perishable cargo not requiring refrigeration. Shown at Collier, Va. on September 13, 1980. *(Robert Reisweber)*

SAL Trailer 30619, series 30402-30901

▼ Here is a view of another Great Dane trailer, this time from the opposite side. Most of the 40' trailers on the SAL were equipped with the "curb door" on the right side to allow unloading at the curb on crowded city streets. The SAL was a tireless promoter of its piggyback service, as evidenced by the striking paint scheme. These colorful trailers stayed around for years after the merger. Shown at Raleigh, N. C. on February 7, 1976. *(Paul Faulk)*

SAL NE 49658, series 49645-49669, class 1CC

▲ There were very few cars numbered in this series by merger time in 1967. This car, built in 1913 by Mount Vernon Car Company, was one of the first SAL cabooses, going back nearly to the beginning of the railroad. As can be seen here, it started the "standard" design that lasted with variations up until the delivery of the first steel waycars in 1949. The safety slogan shown, "Hold Tight 'Til Footing's Right" is correct for all cars ending in the digit "8." Shown in Atlanta, Ga. in December of 1969. *(Bill Folsom)*

SAL NE 49509, series 49500-49549, class 3CC

▼ Originally built in 1914 by Standard Steel Car Company, here is another early caboose. Later cars of a very similar design were numbered in the 5200 series. Early photos of these cars show them with "SEABOARD" spelled out in Railroad Roman type about 12" high, but without the herald. This car shows the standard caboose scheme at Lilesville, N.C. on June 1, 1974.

(Larry Goolsby)

SAL NE 5212, series 5211-5238, class 5CC

▲ This is a nice photo of a wooden sided caboose, rebuilt with plywood sides. Originally built in 1923 by Magor Car, these waycars served up until the SCL merger. They had steel underframes, and were 30 feet long inside, weighed 43,900 pounds, and rode on Vulcan trucks with leaf springs. This car is stenciled with the safety slogan, "Look Around Getting Down," which is correct for all cars whose number ends in the digit "2." Shown somewhere in Florida in November of 1963.

(Joe Klaus, Bill Folsom collection)

SAL NE 5241

▼ Originally built by Magor as a wooden sided caboose, this car was rebuilt as an experiment to investigate the practicality of converting all its older wooden cabooses to steel sides. The double window arrangement on the ends is for a pair of bunk beds. The conversion was too expensive, as this was the only car so done. For years, it was assigned to the Acme, N.C. local, where it survived in service through the SCL merger until the late 1970's. It is presently restored and on display at Hamlet, N.C., were it is shown on February 22, 1988. *(Paul Faulk)*

103

SAL NE 5250, series 5239-5263, class 5CC

▲ Magor built this caboose in 1924. This is the "typical" wooden sided SAL caboose with the standard paint and lettering scheme. The safety slogan on this car, "Tight Grip, Safe Trip," should be used on cars ending in the digit "3." While this car shows some wear, interestingly enough, most photos of SAL wood cabs show every little wear and tear, indicating that they kept these cars up. Shown in Tucker, Ga., in December of 1970. *(Bill Folsom)*

SAL NE 5269, series 5264-5273, class 6CC

▼ In 1924, the SAL went to American Car and Foundry to build these waycars to their standard design, which most SAL wood cabs follow. The safety stenciling for this car, as for all cabooses whose numbers end in "9," is "Rules Obeyed Lives Saved." Note that this paint scheme on this fresh car is slightly different from the previous schemes. Shown in Raleigh, N.C. in September of 1966. *(Warren Calloway)*

SAL NE 5280, series 5274-5303
▲ Here is a really nice slide of a wooden caboose with rebuilt, plywood sides. The plywood gave the impression of steel, at first glance. These cars were built in 1925 by Newport News Shipbuilding to the standard SAL design. This car is shown in Cartersville, Ga. in June of 1969 with the safety slogan that should be used on cars ending in the digit "8." *(Howard Robins)*

SAL NE 5343, series 5304-5353
▼ This is a nice, broadside view of a wooden caboose. A contributing factor to the good condition of these cars, other than good maintenance, was the fact that most of them were assigned to local service, where they did not get as dirty and they were usually under the care of a particular conductor. The safety slogan shown should have been used on cars ending in the digit "1." Shown in W. Palm Beach on March 31, 1968, this car was built in 1926 by American Car and Foundry. *(Eugene Van Dusen)*

105

SAL NE 5412, series 5401-5480

▲ This particular car was built by the SAL to the standard design in 1925. The diagonal steel bracing on the cupola is present on all cars built by the SAL. This particular car has stencil type lettering and the standard safety slogan. Note the red trucks. Shown in Bradenton, Fla. in April of 1970. *(George Eichelberger)*

SAL NE 5458, series 5401-5480

▼ Here is another restoration. This particular car is on display at the North Carolina Museum of Transportation, in Spencer, N.C. The car, acquired by the Museum in 1978, was in fairly good condition. The car is one of several cabooses in operating condition, and is run on a loop of track around the Museum, giving the public the opportunity to ride in an actual caboose. The author provided a set of lettering diagrams to the Museum to assist in the restoration. Shown in July of 1991. *(Dr. Art Peterson)*

SAL NE 5482, series 5481-5482

▲ International Car Company built this caboose in 1952. At that time, this was the standard design being purchased by the SAL for its caboose cars. However, this car, and its sister 5481, were one of two cars purchased by the Macon, Dublin and Savannah as their 600-601. The strange, stacked window arrangement at the end of the car was to provide ventilation for a pair of bunk beds at that location. The SAL cars had an additional window at the top to the left of the herald. Shown at Hamlet, N.C. on February 13, 1966. *(Warren Calloway)*

SAL NE 5483

▼ Here is a fairly unusual caboose in a roster that included just three basic types. This car was originally MD&S 509. While the sides appear to be steel sheets, they are really plywood. The "rivet" seams are nail strips. This car has a centered cupola, and is 31'4" long inside, as opposed to the off-centered style SAL cabs that are 30' long inside. It is assigned to the Carolina Division. Shown at Hamlet, N.C. on February 13, 1966. *(Warren Calloway)*

SAL NE 5604, series 5600-5624

▲ In 1949, the SAL obtained these cabooses, its first steel cabs, from International Car Company. The unusual window arrangement was dictated by the presence of bunk beds. These cars were 30' long inside and weighed 48,300 lbs. Initially used on through runs, these cars were later used in local service. Note the safety slogan, "Watch For Slack, Save A Smack," which is found on all cars ending in the digit "4." Shown in Wildwood, Fla. in February of 1968. *(Paul Coe)*

SAL NE 5619, series 5600-5624

▼ Here is another fine shot of the 1949 series International cabooses. Apparently successful on the SAL, another group of 25 cars, 5625-5649, were delivered from the builder in 1951 and 1952. These were identical to the previous order. Built to a standard International design, similar cars can be found in use on other railroads, including the DT&I, P&WV, and N&W. These cars were rebuilt by the SCL right after the merger into M-6 class 01050-01147, which were similar to the ACL M-5 cars. As a result, color photographs of these cars are rare. Shown in Hialeah, Fla. on October 15, 1966. *(R. A. Selle, Ken Ardinger collection)*

108

SAL NE 5677, series 5650-5699

▲ In 1952, the SAL decided to add yet another fifty cars of the International design to its roster to augment the aging wooden fleet. This group of cars was built by the SAL at the Portsmouth shops from kits supplied by International. They are identical to the previous series. The safety slogan, "A Man At Rest Is At His Best," is used for all cars whose last digit ends in "7." This freshly painted car was found on the cab track at Hamlet, N.C. in June 13, 1966.

(Warren Calloway)

SAL NE 5695, series 5650-5699

▶ This shot shows the original paint scheme of the 5600 series cabooses. Note the black roof. Repaints had their roofs done in red. The safety slogan on this car is, "Long Chances Shorten Lives," which is found on all cars ending in the digit "5." Taken at an unknown location and date.

(John Szwajkart, Warren Calloway collection)

SAL NE 5700, series 5700-5760

▼ Talk about class acts, here is the class car for this series of cabooses. Built by International in 1963, these cars were the "state of the art" for caboose cars at the time. They were 30' long inside, and had cushioned underframes, roller bearing trucks, and nice, high backed chairs with safety belts. They would be the last cabooses the SAL purchased. Note the correct safety slogan for cars ending in "0," "A Man Alert Is Seldom Hurt." Shown in Raleigh, N.C. in September of 1968. *(Warren Calloway)*

SAL NE 5702, series 5700-5760

▲ These cabooses were commonly referred to as "Extended Vision Cupola" cabooses. The design of the cupola was to provide the width of the bay to see around cars while keeping the height of the cupola to see over cars. As such, it was the best of both worlds. This type of car proved to be very popular, serving on a multitude of railroads. Shown in Richmond, Va. in October of 1974.

(Dr. Art Peterson)

SAL NE 5716, series 5700-5760

▼ The extended cupola of these cars forced the modification of the standard SAL paint scheme for cabooses, as the large herald, then in use, would not fit. A 21" herald was attached to the cupola sides. Note the safety slogan of the first car, "Taking Chances Takes Lives," found on all cabooses whose number ends in the digit "6." Shown at Uceta yard in Tampa, Fla. in April of 1974. *(George Eichelberger)*

110

SAL NE 5742, series 5700-5760

▲ Here is a ground view of a brand new SAL caboose enroute to the railroad. Only days out of International at Kenton, Ohio, this car is shown on the B&O at Marion, Ohio on July 21, 1963. The car ahead of it is the 5743, also being delivered. This is a good view of the as-delivered paint scheme. Safety railings and step ends were painted yellow. *(Paul C. Winters)*

SAL NE 5743, series 5700-5760

▼ There is only one superlative to describe this car-WOW! Note that the roofs were painted red, while the running boards remained unpainted galvanized metal. The edge of the galvanized roofwalk can just be seen. This car is shown on the B&O at Marion, Ohio on July 21, 1963. For this car, as for all cars ending in the digit "3," the safety slogan is, "Tight Grip. Safe Trip." *(Paul C. Winters)*

111

SAL NE 5748, series 5700-5760

▲ This nice in service shot shows this car on the rear of SAL's hotshot piggyback train, "TT-23." These cars were used primarily on through freight runs. The dirt on the car is typical for these cars, the result of two years of high speed pool service. Notice the new Fords on the autorack ahead of the car. Shown in Raleigh, N. C. on December 12, 1965. *(Warren Calloway)*

SAL NE 5760, series 5700-5760

▼ What appears to be just another 5700 series caboose is, in fact, unique because it has riveted sides instead of the welded sides of the other cars in this series. In 1965, the SAL decided to rebuild one of the earlier International 5600 series cabooses as a test. The 5622 was chosen and rebuilt with extended cupola and cushioned underframe. It ran around in its old number for a while until it was renumbered 5760. Evidence of this can be seen in the paint patches under the name. The rebuilding program was apparently too costly, for this was the only car done. Shown at Raleigh, N.C. in September of 1966. *(Warren Calloway)*

112

SAL MWW 71976, series 71975-71978

▶ Here is a nice shot of the Atlanta derrick, assigned to Howells yard, cleaning up a spill at Emory, Ga. in May of 1958. The Bucyrus Company built this steam-powered derrick in 1919. This derrick is painted in the standard derrick scheme, which was Pullman green with a herald on the side. Note the cars involved in this derailment, like the round roof cars and ventilator boxcars, as well as the car-load of kraft paper to the left of the derrick. Virtually all the wrecked cars are home road cars. Later this derrick was re-assigned to Tallahassee, Fla.

(Howard Robins)

SAL MWW 71979, series 71979-71981

▲ This is a 250 ton Bucyrus derrick, built in 1945, which was assigned to Hamlet, N.C. This derrick, shown here as steam fired, was rebuilt in 1965 to diesel power. Shown at its home base of Hamlet, N.C., date unknown. *(Wiley Bryan, Ken Ardinger collection)*

SAL MWW 71983, series 71982-71983

▼ Here is the high water mark of Seaboard wreck derricks. Delivered new in 1967 from American Hoist and Derrick, these derricks were slated for assignment at Wildwood, Fla. and Howells in Atlanta, Ga. They were diesel powered. Also shown is derrick tender flat 72567, riding on roller bearing trucks. Note that the derrick tender is also painted Pullman Green. Shown at Hamlet, N.C. in June of 1967. *(Warren Calloway)*

EQUIPMENT CARS

SAL MWD 71722, series 71715-71727

114

▲ Railroads purchased air dump cars for handling dirt and rock to create fills. Most of these cars could dump from either side. In 1945, the SAL purchased these cars from Magor. They were 29'6" long and had a capacity of 30 cubic yards. Shown in Sumter, S.C. in March of 1979. *(Jim Hamilton)*

SAL MWD 71758, series 71740-71759

▼ Here is another type of dump car. Western Wheeled Scraper built this car in 1925. Equipped with arch bar trucks, these cars were 29'2" long and had a capacity of 20 cubic yards. Shown on the scrap line in Tampa, Fla. in September of 1969.

(George Eichelberger)

SAL MWE 71944, series 71937-71944

▲ Another useful piece of railroad equipment is a spreader. The O. F. Jordan Co. made most of them, including the one shown here, so they were called "Jordan spreaders." They were used in spreading ballast, cleaning out ditches, and, in the South, snow removal. This particular model is an older model without a cab. Shown in Atlanta, Ga. on August 24, 1974. *(Bill Folsom, Warren Calloway collection)*

SAL MWE 71945

▼ In 1959, the SAL went to the Jordan Company for a single cab type spreader, shown here. In use, the blades were set at the needed angle and lowered. A locomotive was provided to push the machine. Jordan spreaders were the graders of the railroad world. Shown at Hamlet, N.C. in the early 1960's. *(Warren Calloway)*

116

SAL MWP 71927

▲ This car is listed in the roster as a "crane-pile driver," although here, it looks more like a crane. The Orton Company built it in 1949 as a steam crane, rated at 45 tons. It was originally numbered 71926, and in 1964, was converted to diesel and renumbered. The yellow cab was used on small, yard type cranes. The flat car has been modified for a crane tender. Shown at Ruskin, Fla. in January of 1969.

(George Eichelberger)

SAL TEST CAR 1

▼ Like most other class 1 railroads, the SAL had a fleet of trucks, hi-rail and regular, to service the needs of its right of way. This particular truck was a rail detector car. While painted bright yellow, most SAL maintenance trucks were dark green with a small herald on the door. Shown in Suffolk, Va. on August 30, 1965. *(George Berisso)*

 CAMP CARS

SAL MWX A70233, series A70211-A70233

▲ This is a Bunk-Bath car, converted from an old boxcar, which was originally built in 1937. All Bunk-Bath cars carry the prefix "A." The function of this car was to provide lodging for track crews while away from home. Notice the color of the car, which appears to be boxcar red. Originally, this car was painted Pullman green, but as the paint oxidized, it faded and rusted, allowing the original boxcar red of the car to show though. Shown at an unknown location in March of 1982. *(George Eichelberger)*

SAL MWX A71505, series A71502-A71505

▼ Here is another Bunk-Bath car, also converted from a boxcar built in 1937. This is a good example of how the railroads recycle older equipment for newer uses. Virtually all maintenance of way equipment is rebuilt from older equipment. Note the window variations from the first car. Shown in Baldwin, Fla. on March 28, 1975. *(George Eichelberger)*

SAL MWX AB70690, series AB70678-AB70690

▲ The prefix "AB" means that this converted passenger car is a Foreman, Bunk, Bath car. Among a group of cars purchased from Pullman by the SAL in December of 1947, these cars were never used by the SAL in passenger service. They were purchased and converted directly to MofW ser-

vice. Originally the 12-1 Pullman car *Orion*, it was converted to a tourist car by Pullman in October of 1941. Shown in Savannah, Ga. on July 21, 1973. (*George Eichelberger*)

SAL MWX B70128, series B70128-B70130

▲ This is a straight Bunk car, converted from an old boxcar. Cars of this type carry the prefix "B" on the SAL. The wood sides of this car have held the original green paint much better than metal. Shown at Trilby, Fla. on May 18, 1974. (*George Eichelberger*)

SAL MWX C70784, series C70781, C70784, C70792

▼ This kitchen car was converted from an outside braced boxcar. The prefix "C" stands for "Cook," hence the kitchen car. Note the fishbelly underframe. Shown in Atlanta, Ga. on April 1, 1977.

(*George Eichelberger*)

SAL MWX F70181, series F70181, F70274, F70286
▲ This car is a foreman's car, prefix "F", whose purpose is to provide both quarters and an office for the foreman of maintenance gangs. These maintenance gangs had groups of cars assigned to them, and these cars were moved as necessary to job sites, where they would stay in nearby sidings for the duration of the work. Shown at an unknown location in September, 1974.

(George Eichelberger)

SAL MWX F70710, series F70706-F70717
▼ This foreman car was rebuilt from one of the SAL's many "X-29" type boxcars. Notice the doors in the ends. The steel 1932 design ARA boxcar was the basis of many of the SAL's MofW conversions as time rendered these cars obsolete. Notice the evidence of green paint on the sides, which confirms the original color. Shown in Ft. Lauderdale, Fla. on August 5, 1980.

(George Eichelberger)

SAL MWX G70516, series G70514-G70522

▲ This car, listed as a "two man car," hence the prefix "G." This car was originally built in 1937, and has not been out of the shop long, as evidenced by the condition of its paint. The vents on the roof indicate the presence of baths, and the boxes underneath indicate the presence of propane, which was used for heat. A "two man" car has two bunks, and space for two men, as opposed to four or more. Shown in Ocala, Fla. on February 23, 1967. *(George Berisso)*

SAL MWX J71048, series J71038-J71056

▲ This car is a cook-diner car. Like all cars in this class, it carries the prefix "J." This particular car is part of a group of 19 cars converted from Pullman Tourist cars. Shown in Tampa, Fla. in August of 1979. *(George Eichelberger)*

SAL MWX J71067, series J71064-J71068

▼ Here is another cook-diner car, but this one was converted from a boxcar. The obvious smaller capacity of this car probably made it a candidate for use in smaller work gangs. One can only surmise how hot the interior of this car must have been in the southern sunshine, even with windows! Shown in Baldwin, Fla. on March 25, 1975. *(George Eichelberger)*

SAL MWX K71493, series K71455-K71496
▲ This car, converted from a wooden boxcar, is listed in the roster as a "Commissary-Bath" car. It is one of only 7 cars that remained on the roster by 1966. By the time this photo was taken, this car had been sold for scrap. It awaits the end in Tampa, Fla. in September of 1969. *(George Eichelberger)*

SAL MWX K71497, series K71497-K71501
▼ While this car has the same prefix "K" as the "Commissary Bath" car, it is listed as a "Diner-Bath" car. It is part of a group of cars converted from 1937 boxcars. It is shown in March of 1978 at an unknown location. *(Warren Calloway)*

121

SAL MWX L70098

▲ The "L" prefix indicated a "Foreman-Bunk" car on the SAL. This particular car, formerly Western Union 1211, was converted to MofW service. Even after the conversion, it is still a beauty of a car, with wooden sides and truss rods! It has been said that many MofW crews preferred the wooden cars because they were cooler. Shown in Tampa, Fla. in February of 1965. *(Howard Robins)*

SAL MWX M72171, series M72171, M72173, M72195

▼ Whenever the prefix "M" appears on an SAL MofW car, it has been assigned to tool and materials storage. From the outside, most of these cars appear to be boxcars that have been hastily re-numbered. However, interior inspection often reveals racks and cribs to hold the tools and stores needed on a job site by the MofW crews. The boxcar doors were usually left operational to facilitate quick loading and unloading of materials. The haste in which many of these cars are pressed into this service made them rolling "museums." Shown in Savannah, Ga. on April 2, 1980. *(Paul Faulk)*

SAL MWX M72275, series M72274, M72275, M72279

▲ This tool car has been modified with a pair of windows on the sides to let in light and a coal stove for heat, as evidenced by the roof stack. While one might wonder if the car is still being used as a tool car, the absence of personnel doors on the sides or ends make it unlikely that it is any type of crew car. Shown at Waycross, Ga. on March 29, 1975.

(George Eichelberger)

SAL TA 073152, series 073091-073209

▼ The Seaboard, like most other railroads, did not own many revenue tank cars. They did own a small number of tank cars for use in transporting fuel oil for company use. As such, they ran in dedicated service, and were considered maintenance of way equipment. Cars of both 8,000 and 10,000 gallon capacities were used in this service. Here is an example of one of these cars, which has a 10,000 gallon capacity. Shown in Jacksonville, Fla. in April of 1973.

(George Eichelberger)

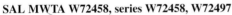

SAL MWTA W72458, series W72458, W72497

▲ Besides being used for fuel oil, old tank cars were also used as water cars in work train service. These cars were used to provide water for toilets, bathing, and cooking for camp cars. This particular car is listed at 8,000 gallons, and is shown in Trilby, Fla. on May 18, 1974. *(George Eichelberger)*

124

SAL MWTA W73248, series W73239-W7324

▼ Water cars, like virtually all cars in maintenance service, were converted from whatever cars were available, so there is a lot of variation, even within the same series. Here is yet another water car, converted from a 10,000 gallon car. Note the dome and the platform that has been added. Shown in Sarasota, Fla. in December of 1972. *(George Eichelberger)*

SAL MWX R70597, series R70594-R70598

▲ This car is one of only five cars listed as a foreman car, prefix "R." These cars were converted from ARA design boxcars originally built by Pullman in 1937. Shown in Baldwin, Fla. on March 28, 1975.
(George Eichelberger)

SAL MWX R70673, series R70663-R70673

▼ While this car carries the "R" prefix, it is listed as a foreman-cook-diner car in the roster. This car was one of several cars converted from old Pullman-Tourist cars, purchased at bargain prices for just that purpose. Shown in Rockingham, N. C. on June, 25, 1977. *(Paul Faulk)*

SAL MWF T72486, series T72473-T72491

▼ Flats are like boxcars in maintenance of way service, in that both are infinitely useful. The SAL recycled its older flat cars for maintenance of way service, as demonstrated by this old, 40' flat loaded with ties. Flat cars were used to haul ties, rail, equipment, tools, and crane tenders. Shown at Tampa, Fla. on July, 1986. *(Joseph Oates)*

![Seaboard Air Line Railroad logo]

COMPANY SERVICE CARS

SAL MWX 72230

▲ This car is one of the SAL's early composite boxcars, which was rebuilt for MofW service, probably as a tool car. Note the ends. While not in the original condition, we can get an idea of what the SAL's early boxcars were like. Shown at Indiantown, Fla. in May of 1970. *(George Eichelberger)*

SAL MWFS 72322, series 72314-72346

▲ This wheel rack car was used to transport wheel sets from remote locations to the Wheel Shop at Hamlet, N. C. These cars were rebuilt from the 99000 series gondolas, which were originally built in 1924. Note the evidence of composite sides and the fishbelly underframe. Shown at Tampa, Fla. in December of 1972. *(George Eichelberger)*

SAL MWFS 72477, series (T)72473-72491

▼ Here is another example of an older MofW flat used as a tool flat. It was originally a older 40' flat car. Note the load of modern track equipment. Shown in Trilby, Fla. in February of 1975.
(Greg Michaels, George Eichelberger collection)

SAL MWF 72515

▲ Here is another old flat, this time with an interesting load! This car is moving diesel trucks to the backshop at West Jacksonville for rebuilding. Shown in Tampa, Fla. in June of 1971. *(Stan Jackowski)*

SAL MWGB 72936, series 72900-72941

▼ This car is a tie car, built in 1940 by American Car and Foundry. Originally numbered 47000-47499, there were 40 of these cars, which were 49'11" long. Like most other maintenance of way equipment, the lasted well into the late 1970's. Shown at Seffner, Fla. on March 5, 1977. *(George Eichelberger)*

MISCELLANEOUS

SAL Brake Car BC-2, series BC-1-BC-2

▼ Needing additional braking power for the Baldwin switchers that worked the Hamlet, N. C. hump and trimmer tracks, the SAL rebuilt a pair of decapod tenders into brake sleds to enable the switch engines to stop long cuts of cars. This sled came from the tender of 532. Later, the concept would be repeated by successor SCL in the form of slug units and road mates. Shown on the scrap line at Rock, Fla. on December 22, 1974. *(Stan Jackowski)*

SAL PO 6602, series 6600-6605

▲ These cars represent the ultimate in SAL lounge cars. Built as Lounge-Tavern- Observation cars, they were originally purchased for use on the SILVER METEOR and the SILVER STAR. Daylight shots of these cars, other than Florida or the Northeast, are rare, due to the nocturnal nature of these trains. This beautiful time exposure of 6602 was made in Richmond, Va., in September of 1966, as it sat in Broad Street Station on the rear of train 57, the southbound SILVER METEOR. *(Bob Yanosey)*

SAL NE 5328, series 5304-5353

▶ Built in 1925 to the standard design by American Car and Foundry, this caboose is shown bringing up the rear of a local. For the last portion of their careers, the wood cars ran in local service. Note the marl in the gondolas, which was being used for new road construction. The safety stenciling for this car, as for all cars whose numbers ends in "8," is "Hold Tight 'Til Footing's Right." Photographed in Sarasota, Fla. in June of 1962.

(Norman C. Miller, George Eichelberger collection)

These two shots, which capture the essence and feeling of the Seaboard Air Line, are used to bid farewell to the railroad, and close our book *Seaboard Air Line Color Guide to Freight and Passenger Equipment*.

The SAL is gone, but not forgotten!